MAKING
COMMON
SENSE
COMMON
PRACTICE

MAKING
COMMON
SENSE
COMMON
PRACTICE

A Leader's Guide to Using
What You Already Know

Victor R. Buzzotta, Ph.D.
Robert E. Lefton, Ph.D.
Alan Cheney, Ph.D.
Ann Beatty, Ph.D.

NewLeadersPress

STERLING &
STONE, INC.

A NOTE ABOUT GENDER SPECIFIC LANGUAGE: Anyone who has written anything longer than a grocery list knows that the English language provides a finite number of methods to eliminate gender from one's writing. We have made every effort to exclude partiality from this book. Our intent was to present a balanced work that demonstrates our high regard for both women and men in management.

Printed in the United States of America on recycled paper.

First Edition
First Printing 1996

CONTENTS

128762

Acknowledgments

A project such as *Making Common Sense Common Practice* requires enormous collaborative effort. For all the support and encouragement along the way, the authors wish to thank . . .

Those Who Helped Us Know Where We Were Going

We are deeply indebted to the 250 executives in North America and Europe who graciously volunteered to be interviewed for this book. The experiences they shared were an invaluable source of inspiration and direction. A special thanks to Ann Buzzotta, director of People Skills International, who interviewed senior executives in the United Kingdom and Ireland thus adding a European perspective to the material presented here.

Those Who Had the Competency to Get Us There

Especially Larry Gross and Bill Hayes who helped put our thoughts, ideas, and early drafts into more congenial prose.

Those Who Kept Us On Track

We proudly acknowledge the contributions made by the people at Psychological Associates and thank all of them for the extra effort put forth to complete this project, particularly to each member of our training, consulting, and sales staffs, whose helpful suggestions and insights kept the authors on track. These included Alan Gerstehn, Rick Glide, Roger Heape, Joe LaMantia, Leo Muelterman, and Bill Piper. We'd especially like to acknowledge the work of Robert Buzzotta, Paula Hawkins, and Dorothy Saeger for their help in shaping the book into an attractive and readable format.

Those Whose Reactions We Trusted

We want to thank the many clients who previewed the manuscript and helped sharpen its message. We want to especially acknowledge Frank Ferrante, vice president, Merrill Lynch & Company, who suggested the title for this book. Mr. Ferrante constantly reaffirms our commitment to the commonsense ideas expressed in this book by using them in the workplace and substantiating their value.

Victor R. Buzzotta, Ph.D.
Robert E. Lefton, Ph.D.
Alan Cheney, Ph.D.
Ann Beatty, Ph.D.

St. Louis, Missouri, USA
July 1996

INTRODUCTION

Why Another Book?

E very year, hundreds of new books are published on business management and leadership. So many, in fact, that *Business Week* provides a bestseller list devoted solely to this category. Many such books attempt to address the people issues that confront today's leaders in the workplace.

These are added to a mountain of volumes already produced over the past decade that are still in print, offering readers advice, counsel, formulas, models, paradigms, systems, and even hugs. They are ready to take managers into the next century or, perhaps, just the coming decade or one minute at a time if they prefer.

Today, the business leader searching for help can turn to a vast, and sometimes unlikely, array of authorities. Titles such as *Leadership Secrets of Attila the Hun, Winnie-the-Pooh on Management,* and *Make It So: Leadership Lessons from Star Trek: The Next Generation* suggest that no stone has been left unturned in the search for the next source of business wisdom. In fact, if a starship captain's cre-

TO OUR READERS: Keeping in mind that today's leaders and managers must often read on the run, we have included "Common Sense Capsules" to accompany the main text. The key commonsense ideas contained in the text are summarized on each left-hand page. This allows you to gain a quick understanding of useful points. We hope you find the capsules helpful.

*A mere generation ago,
leaders could operate with faith that
changes within their organizations would be steady
and predictable. Somewhere in the '80s, though,
big changes started to occur, and all bets were off.
The resulting pressures have required that
organizations reexamine the human side
of what makes for high productivity.*

dentials aren't impressive enough, the ultimate business guru can be found in *Jesus C.E.O.: Using Ancient Wisdom for Visionary Leadership.*

Yet, whether you are a young adult or nearing retirement or somewhere in between, answer this question honestly: How many truly new, bedrock principles have you come across in business or management books since you began your career? Or, for that matter, in life since becoming an adult? Why is it that the human behavior described in the classics such as Homer, the Scriptures, Molière, or Shakespeare is so much like what we have experienced ourselves?

There simply aren't enough new ideas to warrant the number of management books published each year about the people side of business. So, what drives the demand? We believe this turbulent era of business publishing is simply a reflection of the turbulent changes that organizations have undergone during the same time period.

The short list of reasons for the sweeping changes taking place includes competition from globalized markets, shorter product life cycles, and nonstop technological innovation. Yesterday's wish list ideas have become today's lock-down requirements for competing in the marketplace. Producing goods and services "faster, better, cheaper" has become the bottom-line competitive necessity. To be successful, continuous improvement is a must in an unending quest for greater operational efficiency and higher returns for shareholders.

Divestitures and downsizing have been used frequently to achieve asset and cost management. Organizations have been pulled apart and put back together again. Reengineering is the watchword of the '90s as organizations struggle to raise product quality, improve customer service, and achieve optimum market efficiency.

We know that these changes have left many business leaders feeling frazzled and shell-shocked. Perhaps you are among them. After all, a mere generation ago, leaders could operate with faith that changes within their organizations would be steady and pre-

This book has to do with whether an organization's efforts
to deal with change will kill the morale and initiative
of workers or whether, through skillful leadership,
it can achieve high performance by helping people
to respond with the creative energy needed
to carry out its initiatives.

This book will help you tap into what we feel
is the most solid resource you will ever find to face
the challenges of leading people in today's workplace.
We're talking about your own common sense.

Tested common sense has been the mainstay
of generations of successful business leaders.

dictable. Somewhere in the '80s, though, big changes started to occur, and all bets were off. The resulting pressures have required that organizations reexamine the human side of what makes for high productivity.

Consequently, we see the proliferation of books dealing with the people issues as a symptomatic call for help in this new world of change. It's an attempt to get a grip on events, to find a way to feel in charge and be in control of change. For some, it may even be a desperate effort to find a magic formula that will allow those in charge to lead their people and organizations to success, even in the face of tumult.

Maybe *this* novel idea will be the one that parts the sea. Perhaps, *that* new scheme will beat back the chaos and bring order and calm to the workplace. Today's corporate landscape is cluttered—not just with books but also with the remains of agendas, programs, and procedures that didn't remedy our problems. Hence the leap from one new idea to the next, one book to another. Yet something has been overlooked. Something is missing. What ideas can this book offer that have not been put forth by others?

First of all, let's make certain what this book is not. It is not about the nuts-and-bolts business decisions you have to make as a manager. There's no sage advice or wisdom on whether to reengineer, how to change distribution channels, or how to respond to the next technological challenge.

It is about people at work and how and why they contribute to organizations. It is about how leaders can successfully manage people to obtain high performance. This book has to do with whether an organization's efforts to deal with change will kill the morale and initiative of workers or whether, through skillful leadership, it can achieve high performance by helping people to respond with the creative energy needed to carry out its initiatives.

This book will help you tap into what we feel is the most solid resource you will ever find to face the challenges of leading people in today's workplace. We're talking about *your own common sense.* We feel it has been lost in the shuffle. Tested common sense has been the mainstay of generations of successful business leaders. It

Common Sense Capsule

You may be asking at this point why you should read a book about something you already know.

The tried and true somehow seems old hat even though there's much to be said for something tried (or tested) and on target.

has the force of truth because it has stood the test of time. Yet it is as current as today's *Wall Street Journal* headlines because it can be readily applied to whatever new problems or crises arise. We feel totally confident that when this year's hot new solution becomes last year's tired, abandoned cliché, common sense will still provide your best and most viable answer to problems besieging your organization—that is, if you choose to listen to it.

You may be asking at this point why you should read a book about something you already know. If there are no magic answers, no secret formulas to be revealed, what is the point of covering familiar ground?

The answer lies in our subtitle: *"Using What You Already Know."* We are all prone to being intrigued by something novel. The "tried and true" somehow seems old hat even though there's much to be said for something tried (or tested) and on target. In that sense, this book serves as a recalibration, setting our sights on the principles that will serve us well and determining to put them into practice. As you read, we hope we can help crystallize your thoughts, invigorate your thinking, and frame the discussion for applying common sense to the people problems we all face.

Finally, have you ever reread a favorite book at different times in your life? The book doesn't change, but since *you* do, it's amazing how the work seems to provide fresh insights or offer new wisdom. In a similar way, a review of the commonsense principles you already know can be enlightening because you are a leader who is constantly evolving and growing.

By putting the principles of common sense at the center of your leadership role, you will see how to apply tested common sense in the workplace. In a step-by-step process, you can put your organization and its people on a track that will remain straight and true regardless of the changes tomorrow brings. Best of all, you can make it happen without scouring the landscape for a mentor or turning your organization upside down to follow a fad or cult that may not be around for guidance next month, let alone years down the line.

Common Sense Capsule

We hope you will feel as one executive did after reading this text: "The book provided me with a rare opportunity to reflect upon my experiences and get back in touch with what works and what doesn't."

We hope you will feel as one executive did after reading this text: "The book provided me with a rare opportunity to reflect upon my experiences and get back in touch with what works and what doesn't. . . . It's only when we reflect that we, like Dorothy in *The Wizard of Oz,* suddenly realize that what we need, we already have . . . we just need the courage and confidence to use it in an authentic and purposeful fashion."

Victor R. Buzzotta, Ph.D.
Robert E. Lefton, Ph.D.
Alan Cheney, Ph.D.
Ann Beatty, Ph.D.

*Common sense in an uncommon degree
is what the world calls wisdom.*

*The very existence of many organizations has become
dependent on their ability to compete more aggressively in
the face of global competition, to be first in the marketplace
to capture market share, and to reinvent themselves
continually to keep up with technology.*

CHAPTER 1

Common Sense, Change, and Tension

"Common sense in an uncommon degree is what the world calls wisdom."
—Samuel Taylor Coleridge, English Poet

Unless you have been living on another planet, you know that *change* best characterizes what has been happening to almost every organization over the past decade or so. Often this change has been rapid and unpredictable.

The very existence of many organizations has become dependent on their ability to compete more aggressively in the face of global competition, to be first in the marketplace to capture market share, and to reinvent themselves continually to keep up with technology.

It's not as if change weren't around before the '80s, but the pace has accelerated dramatically since then. During an hour-long interview we conducted with the CEO of a Canadian-based multinational corporation, he referred to *change* forty-five times. "You don't have breathing spells any more. Change is so fast that what may have worked well six months ago may not be working so well

1

Out of the fray has come a constant reordering of the corporate entity through divestitures, mergers, buyouts, takeovers, relocations, reengineering, downsizing, and layoffs.

In an effort to mobilize employees and increase their efficiency to meet the crunching demands of survival, leaders have turned to a variety of methods in recent years to manage people better.

You may be discounting your best and most powerful source of reliable management wisdom— your own common sense.

now. You've got to constantly assess and understand the changes occurring around you if you're going to take rapid corrective action."

His comments mirrored what was said by almost every senior executive we have talked to in more than 250 interviews at multinational corporations in the United States, Canada, the United Kingdom, and France.

Out of the fray has come a constant reordering of the corporate entity through divestitures, mergers, buyouts, takeovers, relocations, reengineering, downsizing, and layoffs. Along for this roller coaster ride of change has been the organization's workforce. Every boardroom decision filters down as a people decision that must be addressed by the organization's managers and leaders.

In an effort to mobilize employees and increase their efficiency to meet the crunching demands of survival, leaders have turned to a variety of methods in recent years to manage people better. Quality circles and total quality management programs have been launched. Empowerment and teamwork are more recent attempts to help maximize the contributions made by individuals and groups. Add to these developments the countless motivational books, tapes, lectures, and seminars devoted to improving the performance of workers.

We don't disparage these efforts. We just feel there is an important ingredient being overlooked. As we suggested in the introduction, while searching for dramatically new and different ways to lead, you may be discounting your best and most powerful source of reliable management wisdom—your own common sense.

What are the basic commonsense principles about people and groups that you know to be true? If you can tap in to these truths, if you can take advantage of your own common sense as a guide, you can be a better leader simply by using what you already know.

For instance, it would be impossible to function if you had to approach every person you met without applying rudimentary common sense. You make choices all the time based on your "best guess" as to how people will react. Most of your common sense about others is based on an understanding of human behavior that

You can be a better leader simply by using what you already know.

The principles we will discuss are based on **tested** *common sense.*

All have been empirically verified by psychological research or in the real world of the workplace.

you have assimilated through your experiences in life. Most people feel empathy with others and bring an understanding about them to new situations. Even though you can recognize the ethnic, cultural, and developmental uniqueness of people, your common sense tells you that people are more alike than they are different. They respond with similar reactions and emotions to given situations.

Your own ability to predict the likely reactions of people gets to the heart of our ideas. We are inviting you to trust your common sense and pay heed to it in making leadership decisions. Unlike some of the fads and gimmicks that pass for sound leadership principles, our approach will help you confront the people problems of today, tomorrow, and next year . . . in spite of the pace of change.

This is true because the principles we will discuss are based on *tested* common sense. That is, the assumptions made about human nature have all been empirically verified by psychological research or in the real world of the workplace. They are not the product of armchair experts speculating and manufacturing catchy-sounding theories.

Because we are talking about tested common sense, we are weeding out stereotypes, biases, and prejudices. Some may mistake these for common sense, but they are not; they have not survived testing in the workplace. They have proven to be false.

While it seems logical to apply common sense, leaders often fail to make it a common practice. Let's look at several workplace examples, all of which we have observed firsthand.

Situation

The senior executives of a U.S.-based chemical company pushed hard for employee empowerment. The executives believed it would solve all the problems created by middle-management downsizing, which resulted in the average span of control rising from eight to twenty people per manager. Their direct reports were given more responsibility and encouraged to show initiative. But the results were

*Giving people the freedom to act
should not mean setting them adrift.*

*Common sense says that leaders must help
empowered workers focus their energies
by providing clear direction.*

*Empowerment programs often fail and become
regarded as just another passing "gimmick."*

disappointing. Their efforts seemed off the mark and unfocused. Low-quality decisions abounded. Where was all that creative energy that is supposed to be unleashed when workers feel more "in charge"?

Common Sense

Giving people the freedom to act should not mean setting them adrift. Common sense says that leaders must help empowered workers focus their energies by providing clear direction. True empowerment must be accompanied by explicit objectives. In addition, employees who are "empowered" but not skilled and competent to do their jobs are likely to fail. You can't make people excel simply by giving them the go-ahead. They must have the capability to use their new empowerment; only then will you see its advantages.

What Went Wrong?

Empowerment is not a magic word. Leaders who apply it as a quick fix neglect common sense when they give employees added responsibilities without providing strong direction. They also overlook the preparatory work they must do to make sure empowered people are competent to perform their jobs. For these reasons, empowerment programs often fail and become regarded as just another passing "gimmick" used in management. It's a shame, because real empowerment is an excellent way for employees to develop their potential.

❖　❖　❖

Situation

The U.S. subsidiary of a prominent Scandinavian heavy equipment manufacturer reorganized the production facilities by forming self-directed work teams that would operate without the typical leader. Despite teamwork training, people continued to behave as they always had. They did their parts of the job without touching base with others. They appeared to be competing with co-workers.

*If leaders trying to promote teamwork continue
to recognize only individual achievement,
teamwork will suffer, if not disappear.*

*When change occurs, employees will be more concerned
about themselves than about the firm.*

Common Sense

When leaders introduce teamwork—an alternative to the traditional way of getting work done—they must change their compensation system so that it recognizes and rewards workers for the productivity of the entire team. If they continue to recognize only individual achievement, teamwork will suffer, if not disappear.

What Went Wrong?

While it is admirable for leaders to be innovative in the way they organize workers' efforts, they must follow through and make needed adjustments throughout the system, including how they reward employees. It is just common sense that when workers are rewarded for individual achievement, they will feel they are competing with each other and avoid collaborating.

❖ ❖ ❖

Situation

Competition from larger companies had hurt sales at a U.S.-based pharmaceutical firm, and HMO-type organizations were demanding better quality at lower prices. Management responded by reengineering the production processes. The CEO outlined the new goals and values in a video. The new manufacturing procedures, which were supposed to result in higher quality output at lower costs, also resulted in the closing of some antiquated plants.

Instead of the expected reenergized workforce, management found many employees who appeared anxious and distracted, unable to focus on the challenges at hand. Although costs were somewhat lower, quality also dropped.

Common Sense

People tend to resist change when it threatens their security. "Is my plant the next to close?" "Are we about to be downsized?" Uncertain, fearful employees become cynical and quickly lose their sense of loyalty. Under these circumstances, productivity will most certainly decline.

Common Sense Capsule

*In spite of the fact that most leaders know
how important the human factor is, they let it slip
far down their priorities list as the daily fire fighting
overtakes them. Corporate concerns simply
overwhelm their common sense.*

*Leaders are tempted to respond by looking for new
solutions rather than simply acting on
what they already know.*

*In the world of change, we can be certain that
as organizations attempt to cope, this push-pull effect
between the old and the new will produce
heightened tension in the workplace.*

What Went Wrong?

These executives continued making plans, expecting employees to maintain the same level of commitment to their work in spite of the ominous changes going on around them. Naturally, when change occurs, employees will be more concerned about themselves than about the firm. These leaders should have anticipated dips in production, some defection of loyal employees, erosion of trust, and other unsettling reactions as a by-product of their actions. By doing so, they could have taken appropriate, preventive action to minimize the negative responses, where possible, before they occurred. Wishful thinking or worse, indifference, may have prevented the leaders from identifying with their workforce and seeing the changes from their perspective.

We could give other examples and will do so as we take up individual issues in coming chapters. You can see, though, the pattern of ignoring common sense in each situation. Why do leaders do this? In spite of the fact that most leaders know how important the human factor is, they let it slip far down their priorities list as the daily fire fighting overtakes them. Corporate concerns simply overwhelm their common sense. They tend to forget that so many seemingly new problems are really old ones. Leaders are tempted to respond by looking for new solutions rather than simply acting on what they already know.

Most social and economic forecasts call for a continued lack of stability in the marketplace. So, the commonsense leader must anticipate that the workforce will show a variety of predictable reactions. Some will aggressively fight change and organize resistance efforts. Others will show a dispirited acceptance of the new conditions ("Things could be worse; I still have a job"). Some people will accept early retirement. Still others will "retire" on the job.

Managing Tension

In the world of change, we can be certain that as organizations attempt to cope, this push-pull effect between the old and the new

*In your leadership role, you can and should be
in the business of managing the* tension *level of people.*

✳

*When we speak of tension, we are referring to the catalyst
for generating energy within any system.*

✳

*Peter Senge said, "The gap between vision
and current reality . . . is a source of energy. . . .
Indeed, the gap is* the *source of creative energy.
We call this gap creative tension."*

will produce heightened tension in the workplace. Is this necessarily bad? No. Tension can either be productive or destructive, depending on its effect on people. What matters is how a particular organization and its leaders respond to tension. Why is it that one organization seems tired and immobile, its attitude toward change seemingly embalmed in apathy? How is it that another organization is frantic and distressed, its people easily derailed and almost hysterical much of the time? Why is still another organization able to take on one challenge after another, its leaders and workers energized in their enthusiasm to prevail?

We think the difference in every case is the extent to which leaders are aware of tension and are able to use common sense to regulate it. When you think about it, you can't do a lot about the changes to which your people will be subjected. However, in your leadership role, you can and should be in the business of managing the *tension level* of people.

We are not using the term *tension* here as a synonym for stress. Stress is negative, a nonproductive feeling of anxiety and strain that surfaces when people are put under pressure for extended periods of time.

When we speak of tension, we are referring to the catalyst for generating energy within any system. Tension is present in every human being, in every species . . . even in entire ecosystems. When long-term environmental conditions change in the physical world, they create tension for plants and animals that ripples out like a pebble tossed in the water. Some species are obliterated. Others survive and eventually adapt to the new conditions. Surviving species evolve and even thrive as a response to the tension in the environment.

Tension also provides a catalyst in the psychological realm. In his pioneering book *The Fifth Discipline,* Peter Senge said, "The gap between vision and current reality . . . is a source of energy. . . . Indeed, the gap is *the* source of creative energy. We call this gap creative tension."[1] Tension forms when a gap exists between what we *have* and what we *need* for fulfillment.

13

*Research shows that too little or too much tension
has the same result: suboptimal productivity.*

Between these two extremes lies an ideal level of tension.

*That middle ground of optimum tension is precisely what
the commonsense leader strives to maintain.*

*As a leader, think of yourself as the tension thermostat
for your organization: Your job is to manage productivity
by controlling the tension level.*

Now, apply this to the workplace. Tested common sense says that when there's too little tension in the workplace, employees tend to relax and not take on challenges, resulting in a reduction of effort. Likewise, too much tension creates interference that can paralyze productivity. Workers are distracted by anxiety and stress and are more likely to get sick or have accidents. Research shows that too little or too much tension has the same result: suboptimal productivity.

Regulating the Tension Thermostat

Between these two extremes lies an ideal level of tension. As psychologist Judith Bardwick says in *Danger in the Comfort Zone*, "We don't get involved if the task is too easy or too hard. At its core . . . , creating the conditions of Earning means moving people into a middle range of risk—increasing pressure if people are stuck in Entitlement, or decreasing pressure if they are paralyzed by Fear."[2]

That middle ground of optimum tension is precisely what the commonsense leader strives to maintain. He or she takes the steps needed to raise the tension when it is too low, bringing focused, creative energy back to the task. When there is too much tension, the leader knows how to lower the tension level to minimize its disruptive effects and bring it back to a positive, energizing level.

Figure 1.1 (see page 17) shows the relationship between individual job performance and tension. When tension is too low (on the left), workers lack that reservoir of positive energy that motivates and invigorates. Constructive tension not only creates the resiliency people need to respond to change, it also largely determines how well people perform tasks. Without constructive tension and the energy associated with it, mediocrity becomes the status quo.

Too much tension (on the right) is also bad. It dissipates rather than focuses energy. The level of intensity simply turns tension into stress.

As a leader, think of yourself as the tension thermostat for your organization: Your job is to manage productivity by controlling the

*It is a balancing act. While the right amount of tension
helps people stretch, too much can break them.*

*Just as each individual in the organization
can be gauged in terms of the tension level, so too can
entire organizations. When an organization maintains a
very low level of tension, employees and their leaders do
not feel compelled to achieve productivity goals.*

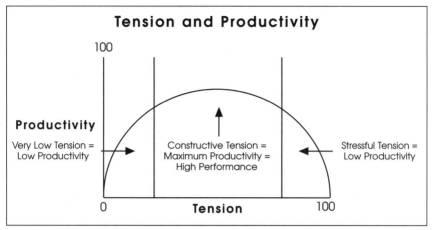

Figure 1.1

tension level. Now when you address the problems of getting the best out of workers during chaotic times, you will have a commonsense overview that crystallizes what you are really trying to accomplish—keeping tension at the optimum level (in the middle). It is a balancing act. While the right amount of tension helps people stretch, too much can break them.

Organizations Also Have a Tension Level

Just as each individual in the organization can be gauged in terms of the tension level, so too can entire organizations. When an organization maintains a very low level of tension (on the extreme left), employees and their leaders do not feel compelled to achieve productivity goals. Jobs are fairly secure no matter how people perform. Employees can feel entitled to job benefits, which often grow lavish over time. Managers may either be aloof or completely accommodating and forgiving. They also feel little motivation to perform. Under these circumstances, no one has a desire to upset the status quo.

If you have ever dealt with or worked for a low-tension organization, one characterized by complacency, smugness, and self-satisfaction, you know what we mean. Such a company can be successful as long as it has a monopoly on the market, product, or

What are the conditions in your organization?
Here are some of the things to look for: corporate strategy,
resistance to change, resilience, and leadership.

technology. However, when conditions change, when the company must compete or strive to find new markets and new customers, its people often cannot collectively summon the energy needed to reinvigorate themselves.

IBM, Kodak, British Airways, Digital Equipment, General Motors, Air France, Sears, K-Mart, NY Central Railroad, Control Data, and Pan American Airlines are all examples of organizations that, at one time or another, faltered because they were slow to respond to change. They seemed almost indifferent and apathetic about responding to the market and their competitors. Some of these organizations managed to turn themselves around while others didn't. The life-or-death battles they waged obviously required them to redefine their strategies. They also needed to redefine their people strategies, to replace apathy with focused energy. In other words, they needed to raise the tension level of both the organization and its employees without creating disruptive tension.

What are the conditions in your organization? Here are some of the things to look for.

Corporate Strategy

Decision makers scan the horizon and see little to worry about. They continue to do what worked in the past, even though changing markets make those approaches increasingly untenable. Decision makers don't anticipate. They don't think about redirecting the organization, which becomes ever more slow moving and cumbersome. Inertia rules.

Resistance to Change

All organizations resist change, but low-tension ones try to smother it, since employees are largely rewarded for maintaining the status quo and are encouraged not to make waves. Thus, change is extremely threatening. That means key people in the organization will actively resist change, aided by the overstaffed bureaucracies typical of these organizations. Innovation is difficult to achieve.

*Let's look at the organization whose level
of tension is too high.*

*Recent history is filled with examples of organizations
that have almost come apart at the seams because
of the catastrophic impact of outside change.
Ironically, some of these organizations were originally
low-tension firms unable to change fast enough to meet
new marketplace demands.*

Resilience

A low-tension organization that resists change for too long may become incapable of changing at all. When outside events finally force a confrontation with new realities, the result is often wrenching, sometimes catastrophic. The organization becomes too rigid to bend. Instead, it cracks, and the tension level spirals upward, sometimes out of control. At this point, the resistance to change gives way to panic and hysteria.

Leadership

Leaders of low-tension organizations have often adopted one of two management styles: hands-off/nonconfrontational or coddling/accommodating. Both ignore or screen out market signals that provide early warnings that change is needed. Hands-off leaders ignore change because it may require them to make hard decisions, such as redeploying or cutting back the workforce. Coddling leaders want to protect high morale and job satisfaction so intently, they deny any evidence threatening the status quo. They won't acknowledge intrusions on their "big, happy family."

Now, let's look at the organization whose level of tension is too high (on the extreme right). As tension increases above the optimal level, stress creeps in and takes over. Why? Because a high level of tension makes employees uncertain and overwhelmed by concerns about their own skills, what's expected of them, and how much longer their jobs will last.

You can feel the tension in these organizations! They operate in a crisis mode. Ironically, because a high stress level sometimes paralyzes workers, productivity falls below what it could be. Sensing that their efforts and abilities have no effect on the organization, that there is nothing they can do to bring tension down, employees do the defensive things people usually do under this kind of pressure. They refuse to take risks and do only what's expected. They withdraw, thereby protecting their emotions and self-confidence from further assaults. They stop caring and shut down.

As with low-tension failures, recent history is filled with examples of organizations that have almost come apart at the seams

*High-producing organizations operate
at an optimum tension level.*

Tension may be high, but the leaders have it regulated.

*Leaders are the regulating thermostats that keep
tension at a positive peak.*

because of the catastrophic impact of outside change. Ironically, some of these organizations were originally low-tension firms unable to change fast enough to meet new marketplace demands. The airline industry is filled with such examples (Pan Am, Eastern Airlines, and others). They imploded, in a sense, sending the tension thermostat needle jumping rapidly from very low to very high. Frequently, they were characterized by leaders who, out of a sense of desperation, applied one "fix it" program after another with tired, hapless, and cynical employees caught in the middle. The result was more uncertainty and turmoil in the workplace.

High-producing organizations operate at an optimum tension level (in the middle). Their leaders have found a way to allow their people to draw a direct connection between their efforts and the productivity, profitability, and overall success of their organization. The tension level is high enough to challenge and motivate but not so high as to be stressful. People see that they earn their pay, their benefits, and job security through their own efforts, individually and collectively. They are aware of what they need to do to keep the organization competitive.

To the outsider, an organization working at the ideal tension level may look just as busy as one suffering from too much tension. The pace may be fast and very demanding. Hours may be long, and many employees may work with a round-the-clock fervor. The difference is a lack of desperation or panic. Their energy isn't misfiring in all directions. Tension may be high, but the leaders have it regulated. They are making commonsense decisions about people so as to lead and direct their energies. They are the regulating thermostats that keep tension at a positive peak.

Notes

1. Peter Senge, *The Fifth Principle* (New York: Currency Doubleday, 1994), 151–53.
2. Judith Bardwick, *Danger in the Comfort Zone* (New York: Amacom, 1995), 63.

Questionnaire

Before you go on to the next chapter, think of your own situation and answer the following questions about how your organization operates. Distribute 100 points to describe your organization's current status.

____ Q1   We believe that we must slug it out in the market-place. We believe strong, hard-hitting promotion is more important than the quality of our products or services. With the right kind of promotion, we can sell the customer anything. We believe we've got to turn the heat up—way up—if we're going to get the most from our employees. When people get burned out, we can always replace them.

____ Q2   We believe there's not much we can do to influence the marketplace. We continue to do things pretty much as we've always done them, including how we reach our customers and the level of quality we build into our products and services. We try not to get our people tense and stressed out about things. We just tell them to do their jobs, don't make waves, and everything will be OK.

____ Q3   We believe that if we have the best product or service, it will sell itself. We believe in keeping promotion and marketing efforts low-key so we don't alienate our customers. Our people not only know that "the world will beat a path to the organization that builds a better mousetrap," but also that contented people are happy and productive people.

____ Q4   We believe that we have to stay in touch with our market and thereby be able to adapt our product, service, and strategy to constant change. Quality of product and service must be in line with marketplace demands. We have to promote fairly and honestly with our customers. We need high-energy people who are committed to achieving the best. Our employees demonstrate both individual initiative and the collaboration required to give our customers what they want.

CHAPTER 2

What Kind of Leader Should You Be?

"Leadership is an action, not a word."

—Richard P. Cooley, American Banker

W ho of the following do you consider good leaders? Do they have something in common? Does each possess a unique quality that makes a good leader? Can you articulate what that is?

Adolph Hitler	Saddam Hussein
Charles de Gaulle	Bill Gates
Pierre Trudeau	Boris Yeltsin
Boutros-Boutros Ghali	Lee Iacocca
Martin Luther King, Jr.	George Marshall
Bill Clinton	Pope John Paul II
Margaret Thatcher	Mother Teresa
Golda Meir	Bob Dole
Queen Elizabeth II	Shimon Peres

Common Sense Capsule

Leaders are visionaries; managers are implementors . . .
or are they?

A commonsense analysis would probably tell us
we cannot afford to have leaders who have little
ability to manage.

Common sense tells us that by fostering leadership
among all personnel, we enhance everyone's capacity
to contribute to the organization's long-term goals.

Unfortunately, it is often hard to spell out a definitive list of a good leader's attributes. In fact, you might find it difficult to list any leadership qualities shared by all the people on this list. Besides, you may not feel they all qualify as leaders. The temptation is to fall back on the gut reaction, "I know it when I see it."

Leaders Are Visionaries; Managers Are Implementors . . . Or Are They?

The distinction drawn in business literature between leaders and managers has clouded the issue in recent years. The idea is that leaders are visionaries, concerned with the larger issues of the organization's purpose and long-term goals. Managers, by contrast, are implementors. Supposedly, managers are only concerned with how to carry out leaders' visions and have no responsibility for leadership.

Proponents of this school say it is important to identify people as either leaders or managers and to separate their roles in an organization accordingly. They would ask which people on our list are leaders and which are managers, who implement rather than lead.

We find this compartmentalizing of little help in addressing the real workplace.

A commonsense analysis would probably tell us we cannot afford to have leaders who have little ability to manage. After all, an organization's vision for the future must ultimately be carried out in the turbulent business environment of the real world. In this setting, our leaders cannot afford to operate on a separate track that doesn't take into full consideration how their vision will be fulfilled. They should be able to help translate any worthwhile long-term goals into specific action plans. In fact, we think those goals will be doomed to failure if implementation concerns are pushed down the organizational chart.

It is equally a mistake to regard managers as strictly implementors, removed from the visionary concerns of the enterprise. Common sense tells us that by fostering leadership among *all* personnel, those who manage and those who do not, we enhance everyone's capacity to contribute to the organization's long-term

A better way to define a leader is to understand how he or she regulates the tension thermostat.

Effective leaders use common sense to regulate the tension and achieve positive results.

Figure 2.1 illustrates four different styles of leadership, by which we can characterize how four different types of leaders will regulate the tension thermostat.

Q1: Autocratic. This style of leadership generates a high amount of tension.

goals. Instead of only one part of the organization being responsible for success, the entire organization is.

A New Definition

We think there is a better way of defining what a leader is that avoids formal definitions, terms, and arbitrary categorizing—a way that provides insights into the real world of work. A better way to define a leader is to understand how he or she regulates the tension thermostat, which we described in chapter 1. Remember, all organizations function with some degree of tension, be it low, high, or somewhere in between. Effective leaders use common sense to regulate the tension and achieve positive results by:

1. Using *both* vision and implementation efforts to engender constructive tension
2. Enabling people to see clearly where they and the organization are going
3. Motivating enthusiastic and focused energy

How do leaders learn to regulate tension in ways that produce these successful outcomes? Whether leaders know it or not, their decisions and actions are always instrumental in affecting the level of tension. So, while they may be *presiding* over a certain amount of tension, they may not be regulating or directing it as a positive force.

One factor that strongly influences leadership style is how leaders regard other people. Figure 2.1 (see page 33) illustrates four different styles of leadership by which we can characterize how four different types of leaders will regulate the tension thermostat.[1]

Q1: Autocratic

This style of leadership generates a high amount of tension. While increasing the tension level can be good for a complacent organization, leaders who show a low regard for people are not able to rally them to consistent, superior performance for very long.

Q1-style leaders overcontrol and insist things be done their way. They apply pressure to wring a performance out of people, not car-

Although productivity may rise in the short run, unfortunate consequences will result.

Workers often burn out or move on.

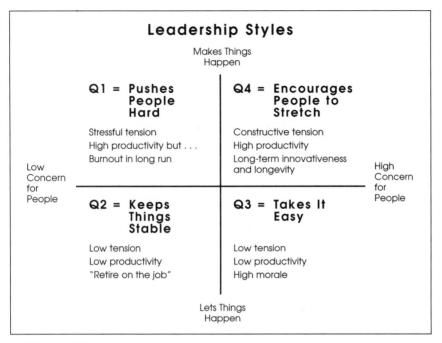

Figure 2.1

ing how people react as long as they perform and meet increasingly higher goals. Leaders with strong Q1 behavior see people only as a means to an end. If employees burn out, so what?

David Mamet's play *Glengarry Glen Ross* is the distillation of every insecure employee's nightmare. It shows a group of shoddy real estate salesmen in a boiler-room operation being given the rules for a new sales contest by their sadistic boss. They are told: First prize is a Cadillac. Second prize is a set of steak knives. Third prize is you're fired.

Does this style work? Maybe for the short term. After all, tension *is* a motivator, even if applied incorrectly. Although productivity may rise in the short run, unfortunate consequences will result. Why? Fear, stress, and panic can activate people to perform, but it uses them up. The inherent disdain shown by such leaders means they invest little in their workers beyond the short term. Likewise, workers quickly invest less and less in return. Why should they "work themselves to death" for uncaring bosses and,

Q2: Uninvolved. Characterized by withdrawing and avoiding overt tension and conflict.

Minimal tension leads to minimal performance.

Q3: Permissive. Leaders exhibiting Q3 behavior avoid raising the tension level in the workplace for fear of creating stress.

The easy self-satisfaction engendered by Q3 behavior tends to undermine optimal performance.

by extension, uncaring organizations? Their performance suffers. They often burn out or move on. Only a steady supply of fresh faces can keep productivity high.

Q2: Uninvolved

Like the Q1 leadership style, the Q2 approach exhibits a low concern for people. However, rather than "cracking the whip" or applying pressure to improve performance, Q2 behavior is characterized by withdrawing and avoiding overt tension and conflict.

The negative effect of Q2 leaders hinders workers in two ways. Because constructive tension remains low in a Q2 environment, those who might otherwise be motivated or challenged to raise their sights are neglected. Their potential lies dormant, and they are robbed of growth that comes from stimulating work. They may be lulled into a satisfied complacency generated by the Q2 leadership style.

On the other hand, those with enthusiasm for their jobs, go-getters who want to play a dynamic role, feel stifled and frustrated by the lackadaisical work environment fostered by Q2 leaders. It's as if a suggestion box hanging on the wall funnels right into a wastebasket below. These workers, so vital to a successful organization, either leave or, worse, adjust their enthusiasm downward. They eventually just "retire on the job."

In either case, the result is the same: Minimal tension leads to minimal performance.

Q3: Permissive

Like the Q2, the Q3 style fosters low tension but for a different reason. Leaders employing a Q3 approach have a high regard for people, so high that they feel compelled to "take it easy" on workers. Striving for a pleasant environment and happy campers, leaders exhibiting Q3 behavior avoid raising the tension level in the workplace for fear of creating stress.

Thus, Q3-style leaders strive for high morale, but not by challenging workers to develop their skills, solve problems, or adopt higher standards. After all, that would create conflict and place demands on people. They prefer traditional low-tension, morale-

Q4: Flexible, Dynamic. Q4 behavior combines a high regard for people with the ability to produce the right amount of constructive tension. This energizes others.

They believe in challenging workers to challenge themselves.

No one's leadership style falls completely within one quadrant, and almost all people show aspects of all four types.

building incentives to motivate them. Pay is high and not tied directly to performance. Benefits are good. Praise comes easily and often.

It is easy for workers to be beguiled in this setting. It's a typical "country club" environment—not that work isn't getting done. It's just that the easy self-satisfaction engendered by Q3 behavior tends to undermine optimal performance, especially if the organization finds at some point that it must raise standards and reinvigorate itself to survive in the marketplace.

Q4: Flexible, Dynamic

Q4 behavior combines a high regard for people with the ability to produce the right amount of constructive tension. This energizes others.

Unlike Q1 leaders, who use raw, positional power to coerce workers to perform, Q4 leaders truly lead by obtaining the understanding and commitment of workers to the purpose and goals of the organization. They "raise the bar" in ways that mobilize people's energy and enthusiasm. In a Q4 environment, people work toward collaborative independence, taking more and more responsibility for their personal productivity.

Q4-style leaders foster high performance based on individual initiative and collaboration. Because they believe in challenging workers to challenge themselves, their "followership" is gained honestly, without dictatorial or patronizing behavior.

No one's leadership style falls completely within one quadrant, and almost all people show aspects of all four types. However, we believe the style closest to Q4 will prove the most successful in today's work environment because Q4 is most apt to maintain the optimum level of tension in the workplace. Referring again to the tension thermostat (see fig. 2.2 on page 39), we can show that the other types of leaders either fail to raise tension to a productive level or cause it to climb so high that a destructive level of stress results. We believe the Q4 style is most likely to regulate the tension that enhances performance and growth.

We believe the style closest to Q4 will prove
the most successful in today's work environment
because Q4 is most apt to maintain the optimum
level of tension in the workplace.

Whichever the case, business has too great a need
for leaders at all levels to rely on destiny
or inspiration to provide them.

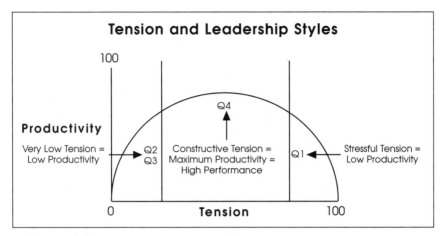

Figure 2.2

Common sense says, then, that the leadership behavior that brings out the best performance of workers is the one to cultivate. But how do you recognize the potential for quality leadership in your organization? How do you find the right people?

Leadership and People Skills

First, some feel that a real leader is "born," not cultivated or trained. In this view, Napoleon, George Washington, Julius Caesar, Martin Luther King, Jr., Mahatma Gandhi, Joan of Arc, Henry Ford, and Lord Nelson were all destined to be leaders, despite where or when they appeared on the planet. However, this view makes it hard to explain the extraordinary leadership qualities exhibited so late in life by Abraham Lincoln.

Others argue that the times shape leaders and call forth their skills. Winston Churchill and Charles de Gaulle might have been footnotes in history had World War II not made them heroic public figures who rallied their peoples against the ferocious Nazi onslaught. Lee Iacocca might not have become a synonym for business leadership without the catastrophe at Chrysler.

Whichever the case, business has too great a need for leaders at all levels to rely on destiny or inspiration to provide them. Plenty of leaders are "made," that is, trained to become leaders. The

*Perhaps, some leaders are born, some are made,
and others become leaders through a combination
of both innate talent and training.*

*Research at Psychological Associates
has identified certain abilities or competencies
required in a leader.*

American astronaut program has done an outstanding job through the years in turning out leaders. Likewise, around the world, business, law and medical schools, as well as military organizations have all trained numerous leaders.

So, perhaps, some leaders are born, some are made, and others become leaders through a combination of both innate talent and training. It is not really important what makes someone a leader. As Donald H. McGannon, an executive with the American Broadcasting Company, has stated: "Leadership is action, not position."

What is important is for an organization to identify the leadership competencies required to achieve its objectives. An organization can develop a leadership profile and measure the potential of its own people and prospective workers against that profile. Only then can the organization make effective human resource decisions: how to hire, develop, promote, and compensate its people—and how to decide who to terminate.

We have proposed that the kind of leader needed in today's business climate is one who can regulate the tension thermostat of an organization, who can effectively direct the constructive tension of its people. We have also suggested that such a leader is dynamic, flexible, and has a high regard for people. The question now is: What specific skills can we look for to find this kind of leadership?

Research at Psychological Associates has identified certain abilities or competencies required in a leader. (These are similar to those identified by other researchers, so they appear to have validity.) According to extensive research, these competencies include:

- Vision, purpose, and direction
- Technical/administrative skills
- Cognition/idea presentation/thinking skills
- Drive and motivation
- Trust and respect (in both directions)
- Teamwork and collaboration
- Ability to empower and enable performance
- Capacity to coach, appraise, and reward performance (give feedback)

*Leadership is not a quality reserved
for top management only.*

*Some degree of leadership is necessary
at all levels of a business.*

We were not surprised that capacity
to coach, appraise, and reward performance *was
ranked as the competency most in need of improvement.
Knowing where they stand is vital to workers.*

Should each leader in an organization exhibit all of these traits? To some degree, yes, particularly since leadership is not a quality reserved for top management only. Some degree of leadership is necessary at all levels of a business. Obviously, not all positions require the same amounts of all eight competencies. To fill any particular position in an organization, we have to develop success profiles, indicating the specific amount of each leadership competency required.

The Leadership Competencies Most Lacking

We didn't list the eight leadership competencies in any particular order. However, we have conducted research to learn how workers rank them when applied to their own bosses. The results are ranked in order from most in need of improvement to least in need of improvement.

- Capacity to coach, appraise, and reward performance (give feedback)
- Ability to empower and enable performance
- Teamwork and collaboration
- Trust and respect (in both directions)
- Vision, purpose, and direction
- Cognition/idea presentation/thinking skills
- Technical/administrative skills
- Drive and motivation.

We were not surprised that *capacity to coach, appraise, and reward performance* was ranked as the competency most in need of improvement. For many people today, this has the most impact on performance improvement. They want to know how well they are doing and how they will be recognized and rewarded. Knowing where they stand is vital to workers.

Feedback is also vitally important to workers because it is used to develop and sharpen personal competencies. During times of dramatic change, they get the message that they must be more flexible and willing to change. So when employees want to increase their marketability as well as prove their worth and chan-

*The second most often cited leadership quality
that workers want to see improved in their bosses
is the ability to* empower and enable performance.

*They want to take responsibility
and to be given an opportunity to excel.*

*The next skill in greatest need of improvement was
to* encourage teamwork and collaboration
among workers' peers.

Least in need of improvement:
drive and motivation, technical/administrative skills,
and cognition/idea presentation/thinking skills.

nel their energies for their employer, they have to know how they are doing. They have to know that both the tangible and intangible rewards that will accrue are clearly linked to behavior that is desired. Only then will they be motivated to improve.

The second most often cited leadership quality that workers want to see improved in their bosses is the ability to *empower and enable performance*. They want the go-ahead to take responsibility and to be given an opportunity to excel. Workers in the survey specified that they wanted clearer goals. They also wanted a clarification of their roles, responsibilities, and authority, as well as the necessary assurance that they would have backing for their actions.

The next skill in greatest need of improvement was to *encourage teamwork and collaboration among workers' peers*. Workers want their leaders to solicit more participation and involvement before solutions are cast in concrete. They also want to work closely with their peers because they feel they can learn a great deal from them. One senior executive at a major brokerage house commented that he has learned more from his peers than he has from any of his bosses, save one.

It is also interesting to note the leadership competencies that workers say are least in need of improvement: *drive and motivation, technical/administrative skills, and cognition/idea presentation/thinking skills*. Apparently they believe their leaders are already working hard, are knowledgeable, and are able to reason clearly and present their ideas convincingly.

But do their leaders understand what people who report to them really want? A number of studies conducted between 1974 and 1994 provided revealing evidence that a gap exists between what workers want and what their bosses *believe* they want.[2] Look at the top three answers bosses gave when asked what motivates their employees and compare the answers with what their direct reports said.

*But do their leaders understand what people
who report to them really want?*

*By believing their employees are motivated chiefly
by tangible rewards, bosses are creating barriers
to their own leadership success.*

*Actually, what workers want are well within the grasp
of leaders at any level in the organization.*

*The remainder of this book explores the techniques
employed by Q4 leaders to motivate people, regulate the
tension thermostat, and foster high performance
within an organization.*

What bosses said:	**What employees said:**
Compensation	Challenging Work
Job Security	Appreciation for
Growth (promotions,	contributions
etc.)	Being well informed

The difference is startling! Notice how the bosses' responses reflect the traditional, paternalistic ideas as to why people work, while workers are focusing on less tangible satisfactions. By believing their employees are motivated chiefly by tangible rewards, bosses are creating barriers to their own leadership success. Why? Because money for raises, opportunities for advancement, and job security have always been in short supply. Since they can't grant tangible rewards, bosses seem to be saying, "There's nothing I can do." In effect, they may be abdicating their responsibility to motivate their workers.

Actually, what workers want—job enrichment, coaching, and better feedback systems—are well within the grasp of leaders at any level in the organization. You have an inexhaustible supply of the very intangibles your workers seek.

The fact is, today's workers are seeking from their bosses what Q4 leadership provides. With Q4 skills, a leader can encourage workers to take responsibility for their own performance and growth and, in doing so, win workers' commitment to the purpose and goals of the organization.

The remainder of this book explores the techniques (illustrated in fig. 2.3 on page 49) employed by Q4 leaders to motivate people, regulate the tension thermostat, and foster high performance within an organization. We believe each of these building blocks is based on a commonsense approach to effective leadership. You will find that each recommendation is sensible, practical, and viable for your own organization. To have a high-performing organization, you need to do the following:

1. *Know where you are going.* Persuade people to commit to a mandate or goal that will give direction and focus to their energies.

Common Sense Capsule

1. Know where you are going.
2. Ensure people have what it takes.
3. Develop and enable the right people.
4. Help people stay on track.
5. Build trust.

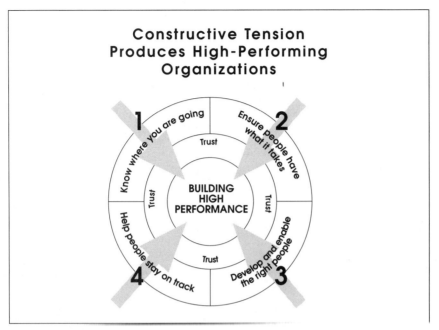

Figure 2.3

2. *Ensure people have what it takes.* Define the competencies required for given jobs and ensure that the people with those competencies are in those jobs.
3. *Develop and enable the right people.* Allow people to take responsibility for their own actions and decisions on the job, within guidelines and limits, after providing them with the opportunity to develop and sharpen the necessary skills.
4. *Help people stay on track.* Develop feedback and reward systems that really tell people how they are doing and how to stay on course.
5. *Build trust.* Trust is the culmination of Q4 leadership in practice and an absolute necessity in today's organization because it's the glue that holds everything together.

Before we begin discussing these leadership techniques in detail, we'd like you to learn a little more about yourself. One of the main tenets of our commonsense approach to leadership is that you become the regulator of the tension thermostat. But what

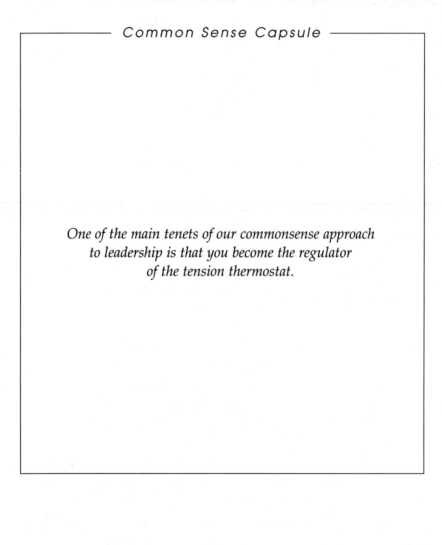

One of the main tenets of our commonsense approach to leadership is that you become the regulator of the tension thermostat.

about your own tension thermostat? If it is not calibrated correctly, it can be an impediment to the process. The next chapter will help confirm that you are reading each on-the-job situation in a clear, objective way.

Notes

1. This model is an adaptation of the Dimensional Model of Leadership Behavior, as described in Buzzotta, Lefton, and Sherberg, *Improving Productivity Through People Skills* (St. Louis: Psychological Associates, 1980), 23-61.
2. "Motivation . . . Different Perspectives," *Board Room Reports,* (October 15, 1994): 4.

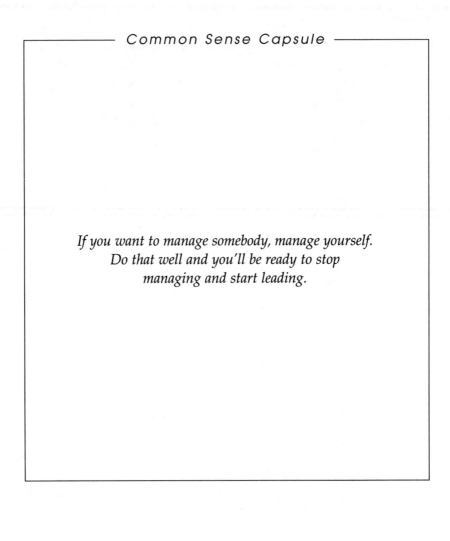

Common Sense Capsule

*If you want to manage somebody, manage yourself.
Do that well and you'll be ready to stop
managing and start leading.*

CHAPTER 3

Calibrate Your Own Thermostat

"If you want to manage somebody, manage yourself. Do that well and you'll be ready to stop managing and start leading."

—United Technologies, *Wall Street Journal*

A department head of an accounting organization has a problem. His boss has come down hard on him because a client is very unhappy about a budget prepared by his department. Word has it this customer is generally dissatisfied and is likely to move her business to another firm. The department head calls a meeting to rally his troops to get new figures together fast. He paces the room, pounds the table, and raises his voice to communicate the extreme urgency of the situation. He becomes resentful because his people appear so lethargic. Why do they seem to just sit there? Don't they know what is at stake if they don't get going?

❖   ❖   ❖

You *are the tension regulator, the instrument that evaluates and manages the tension level of your people. That instrument must be "calibrated" correctly if your perceptions of people are to reflect reality.*

A supervisor is having a sandwich at her desk when an employee bursts in to tell her he just got the latest warehouse and shipping reports and they don't look good. He goes on to say he feels that some new policies have to be instituted immediately or they will lose business. In an impassioned appeal, he pleads for a meeting to work out the details ASAP. The supervisor doesn't know why he is getting so upset. She understands the situation but feels the corporation has always had these problems at this time of year. She doesn't recall a big loss of customers in the past. She tells him these things, trying to calm him down.

❖　❖　❖

A staff manager thinks of his people as a well-oiled machine. They work hard and are able to keep pace with increasing demands. Therefore, he feels confident that everything will go smoothly when he has an opportunity to take a one-week cruise vacation with his family during one of the organization's busiest months of the year. Everything goes well, but he doesn't understand the resentment he senses over his action when he returns.

❖　❖　❖

A supervisor calls a meeting of her staff on Monday morning because she received word late Friday about an assignment that has to be completed by the following week. Over the weekend, she developed her thoughts on how it should be handled and wrote up a proposal. She hands out copies and presents her ideas, emphasizing the timetable. She asks for reactions and finds that no one raises any issues or voices any objections. Assignments to carry out the project are made. Later, as the supervisor enters the kitchen for a cup of coffee, she hears one staff member saying to another, "It will never fly." They both smile and say nothing more. She leaves, wondering if they were talking about her proposal.

*If your own tension level is low,
you may become complacent and fail to respond
to the high tension levels of others.*

*If your state of mind raises your own tension level
out of proportion, you may overreact to what you perceive
as the lethargy and lack of spirit in others.*

In a sense, all of your dealings with people on the job constitute your feedback, the set of signals you receive. This provides the information from which you regulate the tension thermostat in your workplace and make leadership decisions.

In this chapter, we want to explore how your internal state of mind can influence your interpretation of this information. What happens if you are not accurately perceiving the feedback signals your workers are sending? Your state of mind can be a potential obstacle to managing people's performance successfully.

For example, while attempting to regulate the tension thermostat for others, what effect does your own level of tension have? How does it color and distort the information you are getting? Remember, *you* are the tension regulator, the instrument that evaluates and manages the tension level of your people. That instrument must be "calibrated" correctly if your perceptions of people are to reflect reality.

The scenarios opening this chapter demonstrate leaders misreading the feedback they are getting from their workers. If your own tension level is low, for instance, you may become complacent and fail to respond in a meaningful way to the high tension levels of others. Under these circumstances, you may also misinterpret the need for change around you. Your responses to people will be out of sync. You will misread your employees, who may end up feeling misunderstood and resentful. You will find it difficult to put into practice the performance improvements we will discuss later.

The same holds true when the mismatch of tension goes the other way. If your state of mind raises your own tension level out of proportion, you may overreact to what you perceive as the lethargy and lack of spirit in others. This misinterpretation can inaccurately color your evaluation of other people's performance. You may also create destructive tension by your own example. What may be needed in a high-pressure situation is a time-out to calm down, evaluate conditions, and make sure you are managing tension in a way that will focus energies and foster productivity.

*Common sense says that the more accurately you read
your own state of mind, the less likely you are
to distort the reality around you.*

*Why do leaders persist in not seeing how they really
come across to others? Psychological research
and our own observations show that it is difficult to see
ourselves as others see us. When we judge ourselves,
we tend to focus on our good intentions. By contrast,
others judge us by the impact of our actions.*

What You See Is Not Always What They Get

What causes our tension levels to be so different from those of the people around us? There are many reasons our emotional levels can be out of step with our surroundings, not all stemming from the workplace. It really doesn't matter. Just keep in mind that this difference in tension levels can crop up and create a *perception gap,* the difference between how you perceive things and how others perceive them. Common sense says that the more accurately you read your own state of mind, the less likely you are to distort the reality around you.

Perception gaps are easily documented, and they tend to persist. We find that when managers are asked to evaluate their strengths and weaknesses, they typically emphasize their strengths and minimize their weaknesses. If asked to describe the competencies they need to be effective, supervisors tend to describe those competencies they feel they already have. Their ideal self comes very close to what they think they already are. Is this reality or self-deception? They should ask others. Those who work with and under a supervisor have little trouble identifying shortcomings as well as strengths.

Why do leaders persist in not seeing how they really come across to others? Psychological research and our own observations show that it is difficult to see ourselves as others see us. When we judge ourselves, we tend to focus on our good *intentions.* By contrast, others judge us by the impact of our *actions.*

Fall Into the Gap

Over time, there is another profound consequence for leaders who are unable to see the gap between their idealized views of themselves and their actual behavior. Think of the personal tension thermostats of supervisors who are content with their performance. They see no need to renew their sense of purpose or challenge themselves to improve because they are blocking out the stimulus for constructive, creative tension. They become stuck in

As they climb the executive ladder,
managers receive less and less reliable feedback.

While many criticized President John F. Kennedy
for appointing his brother to an important
Cabinet position, he saw it as a way to get feedback
from someone who would not be intimidated
by his position.

We think you must vigorously seek self-correcting,
authentic feedback.

time, petrified, doomed to repeat the same mistakes. They become poor leaders.

A leadership style that is set in cement is a particular hazard for people in senior management. As they climb the executive ladder, managers receive less and less reliable feedback. If they don't guard against it, they not only receive fewer signals (since fewer people have access to them), but the signals they do receive also become less reliable. A low state of creative tension is rarely challenged since upper management is often surrounded by sycophants who are hesitant to be candid. We're all familiar with the humorous portrayal of "yes-men" on TV and in film.

The history of royalty and other heads of state can be viewed as an elaborate game of who has the throne's ear. The same can occur in the upper echelons of business if care isn't taken to keep it from happening. While many criticized President John F. Kennedy for appointing his brother to an important Cabinet position, he saw it as a way to get feedback from someone who would not be intimidated by his position, someone he could trust to level with him.

Mirror, Mirror on the Wall

Given the elusive nature of what's really happening out there, are you trapped by your own subjective take on the world? How can you step outside of yourself and be free from distortions that create a potential gap between your perceptions and reality? We think you must vigorously seek *self-correcting, authentic feedback.*

Simply being aware of the perception gap problem should prompt you to look around and evaluate situations better. The leaders in our four examples were not picking up incoming signals accurately. Remember, everything around you is a source of feedback. It includes the broad range of input you receive at work: praise, criticism, official compensation, performance reviews, the size of your office, even how people smile at you when you pass them in the hall.

How well you notice signals depends on how sensitive you are to them. Some leaders have strong "antennae" and soak up more self-correcting information from a wider variety of sources than

Some leaders have strong "antennae" and soak up more self-correcting information from a wider variety of sources than others. Some seem never to notice adverse signals.

The organization may distort the feedback.

Accepting feedback is difficult for anyone, but it is even harder for people who have enjoyed successful careers.

others. Some seem never to notice adverse signals, usually to their eventual peril. There are several common reasons for distortion that can challenge anyone trying to get authentic feedback.

First, the organization may distort the feedback. Think of a workplace that cultivates a lot of Q3 leadership (overly positive, keep everyone happy). There you could be as deceived as anyone else by being praised by a boss who doesn't really mean it or rewarded for a performance that doesn't warrant it. In these entitlement organizations, "feel good" performance reviews are expected, pay raises are automatic, and benefits are expanded without regard to real growth or improvement. Instead of being authentic, it is all false-positive feedback.

Another problem is that negative feedback about ourselves is not easy to accept. No one likes bad news, and when you solicit authentic feedback, some will no doubt be negative. Typically, when confronted with uncomplimentary feedback, our first reaction is to feel discomfort. This rise in tension may trigger anger and the desire to deny the information's validity. This may lower tension, but it also lowers the desire to change and improve. Denying or rationalizing will only mean a return to the very behavior that should have been singled out for change.

Accepting feedback is difficult for anyone, but it is even harder for people who have enjoyed successful careers. Consider an executive who has risen in the organization because of a particular talent. Perhaps he or she is a financial expert, a technical genius, or marketing whiz. At the same time, this person has always exhibited strong Q1 behavior. How likely will he or she feel the need to change leadership behaviors?

In the 1960s, we worked with the CEO of a highly profitable, major transportation company who was a brilliant but autocratic leader, exhibiting a very typical Q1 style. This high-powered executive wondered what the pre-employment psychological tests used by his HR group might have to say about him. He arranged to take the pencil-and-paper inventory designed to identify leadership characteristics. He then asked his vice president of HR to interpret the results. With understandable trepidation, the HR

360-degree feedback: candid feedback from people who work all around you.

Many CEOs and senior executives we have worked with use this method to ensure they receive the candid feedback they need to recalibrate their own tension thermostats.

In the thousands of development programs we've conducted over the years, we've found that the majority of our participants are eager to receive candid, constructive feedback.

executive gave it to the CEO straight. The inventory showed that the CEO was bullheaded and close minded, thought he was always right, frequently made unrealistic demands, and in short tended to demean others and grind those around him into the dust.

"Interesting," the CEO said. "But, tell me. Doesn't it say anything *bad?*"

Needless to say, it would be next to impossible to convince this person that he needed to change. He undoubtedly felt the aggressive way he had behaved as a leader was part of his formula for success. Unfortunately when the nature of the transportation industry changed drastically, he became increasingly out of touch with the realities his company faced, and eventually the board of directors replaced him.

Besides understanding the roadblocks that inhibit receptiveness to feedback, we must also ensure that the feedback we are receiving is authentic. An excellent method we have used involves 360-degree feedback. This procedure solicits anonymous, candid feedback from people who work all around you—your boss, fellow managers, direct reports, perhaps even customers. Information is direct, organized, and thorough. It also provides a detailed profile of how others see you. It confronts the perception gap head-on. Many CEOs and senior executives we have worked with use this method to ensure that they receive the candid feedback they need to recalibrate their own tension thermostats.

There's a prevailing feeling that people don't want candid feedback, but our experience indicates just the opposite. In the thousands of development programs we've conducted over the years, we've found that the majority of our participants are eager to receive candid, constructive feedback that can be used to set self-development priorities. When we ask the participants of our leadership development seminars to describe the highlights of the experience, 70 to 80 percent select the feedback exercise built into the course.

As leaders, our job is to help regulate the level of constructive tension of our workers. We must be certain our own thermostat is reliable and calibrated correctly. Soliciting feedback is the most

Common Sense Capsule

We must be certain our own thermostat is reliable and calibrated correctly. Soliciting feedback is the most dependable way to keep it accurate.

dependable way to keep it accurate. Remember, it is an ongoing process.

As we proceed, we will reveal the commonsense techniques necessary to regulate the level of constructive tension within an organization. We will explain how these techniques work and show why they are the key to maximizing productivity.

The time: 11:30 P.M.
The place: The intensive care unit at City Hospital.

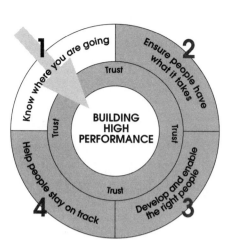

CHAPTER 4

Know Where You Are Going

"The great thing in this world is not so much where we stand, as in what direction we are going."

—Oliver Wendell Holmes, American Author and Physician

The time: 11:30 p.m. The place: The intensive care unit at City Hospital.

Nurse Jenkins notices an irregularity on the monitor of the patient in room 301—a dangerous heart rhythm. He flips on the intercom: "Code blue, room 301."

Jenkins calls for the emergency crash cart. He then reports to the patient's room and begins CPR treatment, assessing the patient's breathing and circulation.

The floor supervisor arrives, then a respiratory therapist. The three remove the headboard from the bed, turn the patient, and place the board beneath him for support. The doctor on call arrives, as well as a nurse trained in advanced cardiac life support.

Businesses, too, face crises. Think of the Tylenol tamperings, the bankruptcy at Barings, the flawed Pentium chip, and the Exxon Valdez *disaster.*

Tension can focus energy to accomplish an organizational objective.

One team member documents everything on a clipboard while others continue CPR, performing chest compressions and mouth-to-mouth resuscitation. Pulse and blood pressure are continually monitored. Medications and oxygen are readied. The defibrillator is brought in from the crash cart.

The doctor assesses the patient's vital signs, interprets the heart monitor, and selects one of ten treatment scenarios. She orders defibrillation. A nurse steps forward with the defibrillator paddles, commands "Clear!" and applies them to the patient's chest.

The time is now 11:31 P.M.

Although the hospital room is full of tension, an orderly and knowledgeable response occurs with this cardiac crisis. While not an example of a crisis from the world of business, it is a dramatic example of how tension can produce positive, constructive energy that galvanizes every member of a team to work toward a clearly defined purpose.

Businesses, too, face crises. Think of the Tylenol tamperings, the bankruptcy at Barings, the flawed Pentium chip, and the *Exxon Valdez* disaster. Calamities like these produce tension. Yet, much like the ER team's response, such tension can focus energy to accomplish an organizational objective.

If You Don't Know Where You Are Going, Any Road Will Get You There

In the summer of 1994, Northwest Airlines made an unusual offer to the public. For fifty-nine dollars, travelers could take a flight for one day from Indianapolis to any city in the United States served by the airline. However, there was one catch: Passengers were not told which city they would fly to until they arrived at the airport, shortly before their flight departed.[1]

Three hundred people quickly snatched up Northwest's cut-rate ticket offer, people with spare time who wanted to go somewhere just for fun, as a lark. You wouldn't have expected businesspeople

Businesses often send messages throughout their organizations that their personnel are on flights to unknown destinations.

Ambiguity results in tension that is either too low or too high.

We believe leaders have three fundamental ways they can involve every employee and show each customer and supplier what the organization is about: a clearly defined vision, mission, and set of values.

to be among those buying tickets, hoping that pure luck would land them in a city to their benefit.

Yet businesses often send messages throughout their organizations that their personnel are on flights to unknown destinations. Their leaders fail to state an explicit purpose and direction. Perhaps it is supposed to be obvious to everyone where the organization is going. However, this is a risky assumption in today's turbulent business climate.

Unfortunately, the lack of a clear, purposeful destination often fosters nonproductive levels of tension. Common sense tells us that ambiguity cannot be translated into useful action. Ambiguity results in tension that is either too low or too high. As people try to function without knowing where their organization is going, they may develop the lackadaisical attitude, "Why worry?" Or an information vacuum may develop. Workers will then project their worst fears into it, and tension can spiral out of control and become stress.

That's why a clearly communicated sense of purpose and direction is needed to keep people focused. This specific focus generates an environment that can harness everyone's energy to achieve the objectives of the enterprise.

How Do We Get There from Here?

What methods are the most effective for generating a sense of purpose and direction throughout an organization?

We believe leaders have three fundamental ways they can involve every employee and show each customer and supplier what the organization is about: a clearly defined vision, mission, and set of values.

Cultivate Your Vision

In our society, many neglect the idea of vision as not being bottom line enough for business. It doesn't show up on the P&L statement. It seems too intangible, too conceptual, too . . . visionary! Remember President George Bush being annoyed by critics who kept asking him about "the vision thing"?

If your goal is to harness the energy of all personnel to develop an effective, high-performing organization, then you and your organization need a strong sense of vision.

A vision is a compelling mental image of an extraordinary accomplishment goal the organization sets for itself that raises the sights of its members.

In 1960, John F. Kennedy proclaimed his vision: "I believe this nation should commit itself to achieving the goal, before the decade is out, of landing a man on the moon and returning him safely to earth."

Indeed, it appears that many organizations function without a vision. The day-to-day and even year-to-year activities of a firm seem to roll along of their own momentum. However, if your goal is to harness the energy of all personnel to develop an effective, high-performing organization, then you and your organization need a strong sense of vision. It helps ensure that everyone is pulling in the same direction. It serves as a clarion call to rally the troops.

What is a vision? A vision is a compelling mental image of an extraordinary accomplishment goal the organization sets for itself that raises the sights of its members. It is a beacon that cuts through the day-to-day activities, allowing everyone to stay focused on the big picture while accomplishing individual tasks.

For example, the U.S. space program in the 1950s wanted to catch up with the accomplishments of the Soviet Union. In 1960, John F. Kennedy acted to mobilize and unify the people of NASA by proclaiming his vision: "I believe this nation should commit itself to achieving the goal, before the decade is out, of landing a man on the moon and returning him safely to earth."

That simple declaration became a guiding spirit, pointing the direction for everyone working in the space program. There was no doubt over the next nine years what every meeting, every proposal, every budget, every decision was ultimately intended to accomplish.

If we can communicate our vision and persuade the members of the organization to become a part of it, we will raise the collective constructive tension. The problem is that over time and because of the press of day-to-day activities, we can not only forget to communicate our vision, but we may also lose a clear sense of what it is.

It's no accident that early on in their existence, organizations often have a strong vision to guide them. Their founders have a compelling reason and strong motivation for beginning their enterprises. History is filled with examples of the dedication of forceful personalities who began successful ventures because they formulated a singular vision of what they wanted to accomplish.

History is filled with examples of forceful personalities who began successful ventures because they formulated a singular vision of what they wanted to accomplish.

Henry Ford: "A car every working man can afford."
Bill Gates: "A PC on every desk and in every home."

Almost every successful organization early on develops a strong sense of what it wants to be.

Avis: "We're Number Two. We try harder."
British Airways: "The world's favorite airline."

Henry Ford: "A car every working man can afford."
Bill Gates: "A PC on every desk and in every home."
Walt Disney: "A magical little park to amuse and
educate both children and their parents."

While not all organizations' founders formulate visions as striking as these, we believe almost every successful organization early on develops a strong sense of what it wants to be.

Here are several examples of the brief but often elegant vision statements that have guided organizations with many thousands of members.

Sears: "Quality at a good price."
Avis: "We're Number Two. We try harder."
British Airways: "The world's favorite airline."
The Girl Scouts: "To help girls grow into proud, self-
confident, and self-respecting women."

Could these organizations function without visions to point people in the right direction? Maybe. But we have witnessed over the past several decades any number of strong organizations that have lost their way because they didn't hold onto the compelling image of why they existed, what they were striving to achieve.

We are not saying the vision must be chiseled in stone and stand for the next hundred years. Nor are we suggesting that leaders should shop around, adopt a vision, and slap it into place. The point is that we believe there *is* a vision for your organization, even if it hasn't been articulated. It comes from within. Determining what you want your organization to accomplish overall and then verbalizing it to all employees serves not only to focus their actions but also to inspire them. The people working in the space program in the 1960s accomplished complex and difficult tasks they had not dreamed possible. That's the power of a vision to motivate and unleash boundless constructive tension.

The benefit of having an articulated vision in place is that the person employed to perform even the most elementary tasks is not just a hired hand but also a partner in achieving the organization's overall goal. At the very least, instead of allowing three hundred

*A vision clearly states where you want to go
and invites everyone to get on board.*

*The substance of the statement should assert
what the enterprise can be at its best.*

*If the vision of an organization serves to
unite its people by pointing to its destination,
the mission specifies how they will get there.*

*In a way, the mission is the prose to the vision's poetry.
A well-formulated mission states concisely
the who, what, and why.*

people to hold tickets to different destinations, a vision clearly states where you want to go and invites everyone to get on board.

What does it take to construct a vision statement that conveys the sense of what your organization is trying to accomplish? The substance of the statement should assert what the enterprise can be at its best. Or it should direct people toward the solution to a problem. It may also articulate the overreaching goals of the enterprise—what should be achieved in the long run. The statement itself will be concise, motivating, and memorable. It defines your organization's uniqueness.

Develop a Mission

If the vision of an organization serves to unite its people by pointing to its destination, the mission specifies how they will get there. The mission is similar to the vision of an organization in that it is the expression of an ideal, a goal for which all employees should strive. Also like a vision, a mission enlists employees to be more than interchangeable parts in the machinery of the organization. The mission enrolls them as contributors, all pulling in the same direction.

In a way, the mission is the prose to the vision's poetry. A well-formulated mission states concisely the who, what, and why. It spells out for each employee (and the public at large) the goals the organization wants to reach. It specifies at minimum the type of business it is, its markets, its customers, and its financial goals. To be effective, the process of developing the mission entails a thorough and candid evaluation of the organization and its competitive environment. It also expresses the aspirations of its leaders.

Unlike vision statements, which by definition are short, mission statements may vary in length, from a couple of paragraphs to several pages.

The Ritz-Carlton Hotel chain's vision statement is brief: "We are ladies and gentlemen serving ladies and gentlemen." The mission, on the other hand, elaborates on how employees will conduct themselves.

Common Sense Capsule

*The Ritz-Carlton Hotel chain's vision statement
is brief: "We are ladies and gentlemen serving
ladies and gentlemen." The mission, on the other hand,
elaborates on how employees will conduct themselves.*

*Common sense tells us that organizations cannot
be everything to everyone. It is unlikely that
all of the following can be achieved by one entity:
low-cost provider; product superiority; and
outstanding, personal customer service.*

*To help crystallize the commitment of
everyone in your organization, formulation should
involve as many people as possible.*

The Ritz-Carlton Hotel is a place where the genuine care and comfort of our guests is our highest mission.

We pledge to provide the finest personal service and facilities for our guests who will always enjoy a warm, relaxed yet refined ambiance.

The Ritz-Carlton experience enlivens the senses, instills well-being, and fulfills even the unexpressed wishes and needs of our guests.

While the Ritz-Carlton changes its specific operations from time to time, its mission successfully conveys what the organization expects each person working at its hotels to achieve. Each employee also understands what is expected. The mission points the way and sets a proud standard for performance. In addition, such a strong mission statement allows the organization to develop its operational regulations and guidelines to be consistent with its goals.

Another part of a mission's value is to define its expectations, for example, in the marketplace. Common sense tells us that organizations cannot be everything to everyone. It is unlikely that *all* of the following can be achieved by one entity: low-cost provider; product superiority; outstanding, personal customer service. An organization's mission must specify which of these three is preeminent. If product superiority is its chosen niche in the marketplace, then the organization will have to focus its effort on research and development. If its goal is to be the low-cost provider, it may need to focus on sharper buying and low-cost distribution. Discount retailers are good examples. If, on the other hand, its niche is outstanding personal customer service, it will emphasize the selection and training of its personnel.

We have touched only briefly on how a vision and mission serve as excellent tools to stimulate leaders to think about an organization's purpose and direction. There are a number of good resources and publications that can help with the specific formulation of vision and mission statements. Remember, though, because the purpose is to help crystallize the commitment of everyone in

When a gap exists between what leaders say and what they do, nonconstructive tension results.

Why should they make a fundamental commitment to principles and goals not honored and practiced by their leaders?

your organization, formulation should involve as many people as possible.

Mission Accomplished?

Articulating a vivid and compelling picture of where the enterprise is headed is just the beginning. The vision and mission statements do not become magical mantras to be intoned in ritualistic fashion. Executives who view the development of a vision or mission statement simply as an exercise, something handsome to frame and hang on the wall of the reception area, are missing the point.

Rather, these statements must be brought to life through clear, understandable communication and a commitment to behave according to their principles.

Employees will quickly see through a program cooked up by the PR department as a substitute for meaningful commitment. Posting slogans and banners or making "rah rah" speeches will not induce desirable behavior for very long.

When a gap exists between what leaders say and what they do, nonconstructive tension results. Employees become cynical, withdraw their commitment to the vision, and stop paying attention to the mission. Why should they make a fundamental commitment to principles and goals not honored and practiced by their leaders?

On the other hand, when employees recognize that everyone in the organization, beginning with those at the top, is willing to personify the organization's stated beliefs, an environment of positive creative tension is cultivated. Real enthusiasm and dedication are possible.

Look at Healthtex, a children's clothing firm in the United States. It had become unprofitable and was on the verge of failure as its market changed. In 1990, when its leaders decided to examine the fundamental purpose of the business and define its customers and mission, the company experienced a dramatic turnaround.

Crafting a highly strategic mission statement helped establish a common direction for various groups within the organization. As

What will guide the behavior of your organization in its day-to-day decisions?

The answer lies in your organization's values.

Corporate values express the ethics that guide an organization's behavior as it goes about achieving its mission.

If you think of vision and mission as an organization's head and heart, the values it holds are its soul.

Healthtex's president Gary E. Simmons stated, "The goal here is that everybody—be it a machine operator, a designer, or the head of human resources—is thinking in a similar vein. It doesn't mean they all think alike, but at least they all have a central core belief of what our organization is trying to achieve."[2]

By 1994, the people at Healthtex had posted a 40 percent increase in profits two years in a row. Try telling the people there that developing a clear, common direction wasn't a valuable exercise!

Execute with Values

Beyond knowing where you are going and how you will get there, what will guide the behavior of your organization in its day-to-day decisions? How will it behave toward those with whom it comes into contact—its customers, its employees, its stockholders? The answer lies in your organization's values.

In a recent article published by the Center for the Study of American Business, the CEO of Corning, Incorporated, James R. Houghton said, "I think of values as buoys in the channel of commerce. For 145 years they've helped keep us headed in the right direction as we've made the necessary course corrections in the ever-changing sea. They continue to guide us as we make the millions of decisions that must be made to run the enterprise—decisions that will be better because they are constantly tested against our values."

Corporate values express the ethics that guide an organization's behavior as it goes about achieving its mission. You can find a story in the newspaper almost every day that calls into question a corporation's values. When you read these stories, it becomes obvious that values (or the lack of them) are an integral part of the identity of an organization, its reason for being and its destination. If you think of vision and mission as an organization's head and heart, the values it holds are its soul.

And they don't come from the bottom up. Corporate values must have the commitment of the organization's leadership. The

*A strong set of values provides every member
of an organization with guidelines required to decide
what to do. This encourages creative tension
because values point the way to the appropriate
course of action when problems arise.*

values should be easily understood and simple to transform into action by everyone.

Merrill Lynch, one of the world's largest brokerage houses, for example, developed five commonsense values to guide their actions: client focus, integrity, teamwork, respect for the individual, and responsible citizenship. Merrill Lynch chose these values to serve as a foundation for its organizational and employee practices as the result of solid, commonsense thinking.

Common sense demands that any organization must *focus on the customer* if it expects to succeed in the marketplace. Satisfying the needs of customers must be central to everything it does. *Integrity* is absolutely vital if we are to establish trust and confidence among our employees and customers. Customers want to buy from people they trust, and employees are more willing to collaborate when they trust the organization. This makes *teamwork* possible, which consolidates people's knowledge and talent, promotes innovation, and produces the solutions to meet customer needs. It also makes sense that individuals are more apt to collaborate when they feel their ideas and contributions will be treated with respect. Thus, *respect for the individual* allows people to develop their potential fully.

Finally, our employees and customers live in the community in which we operate. Through *responsible citizenship,* we show consideration and support for the ideas and institutions that are important to them.

Without values, employees can be unsure about the decisions they are called on to make and the actions they must take. Destructive tension can result from this lack of information. The absence of continuity and consistency within an organization creates a feeling of being adrift.

On the other hand, a strong set of values provides every member of an organization with guidelines required to decide what to do. This encourages creative tension because values point the way to the appropriate course of action when problems arise. Think of the values of Johnson & Johnson, which guided a swift and honest response to the Tylenol tampering crisis a few years ago.

Today, every employee at every level of the organization carries a pocket card that enumerates what he or she promises to do to achieve the company's goals.

Commonsense leaders chart a clear course: "Here's where we're going. It's time to get on board or be left behind."

The Sum Is Greater Than Its Parts

When an organization puts it all together—an uplifting vision, a strong mission, and meaningful values—and then communicates all three loudly and frequently, its members are enrolled in the purpose and direction of the organization.

A major international oil company with whom we have worked serves as a case in point. The leaders of the enterprise developed an explicit vision, a mission statement, and a list of values and corporate objectives. They asked all employees to translate the corporate statements of purpose and direction into specific, individual commitments. Today, every employee at every level of the organization carries a pocket card that enumerates what he or she promises to do to achieve the company's goals. That's working with a sense of purpose!

Commonsense leaders chart a clear course: "Here's where we're going. It's time to get on board or be left behind." Those who do not fully agree with that direction are forced to choose between realigning and redefining their roles and activities or leaving the organization.

For those who stay, a clear direction mobilizes energy by raising the constructive level of tension. It leads to focused action.

Cultivating a vision, a mission, and values should not be looked at as an assignment to get out of the way before moving on to more important matters. Instead, view them as the starting point for a high-performance organization. They serve as a foundation for the steps we build on in the following chapters. The stronger your sense of where you are headed, the better your decisions will be about deploying your resources—especially your people, as you will see in the next chapter.

Notes

1. "300 Travelers Snatch Up NWA Mystery Fares," *Travel Weekly* (August 29, 1994): 1.
2. "Mission Statement Provides a Focus for a Company— Whatever Its Size," *Nation's Business* (February 1994): 62.

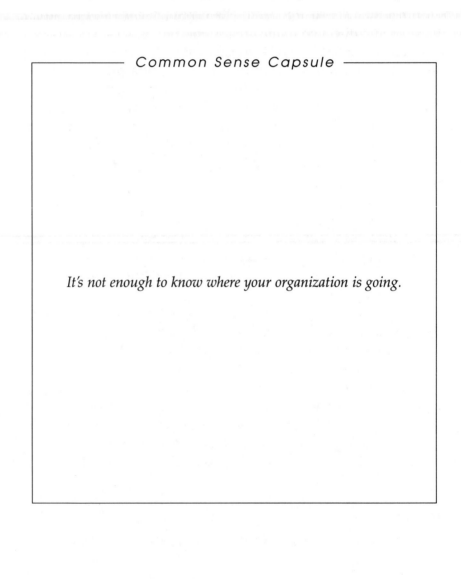

— Common Sense Capsule —

It's not enough to know where your organization is going.

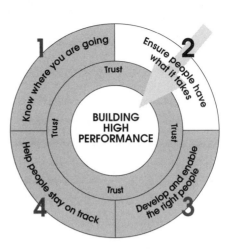

CHAPTER 5

Ensure People Have What It Takes

"No duty the Executive had to perform was so trying as to put the right man in the right place."

—Thomas Jefferson

It's not enough to know where your organization is going. Once you create a worthy vision, clarify your mission, and operate with enlightened values, common sense says that some other vital changes will have to take place.

The coming of Prohibition in the United States during the 1920s provides extreme examples of organizations whose missions were abruptly redirected. Overnight, the breweries, distilleries, and wineries of America found themselves involved in ventures that were declared illegal. Their products had been outlawed.

Surprisingly, many of these companies did manage to survive that social experiment, and they continue to do business today. Some took advantage of their bottling capabilities and became soft drink manufacturers. Others put to use their expertise in the grain

*Charting a new course always dictates that adjustments
in an organization's structure be made.*

*Some of the old job slots will require redefinition.
Likely, entirely new jobs may have to be created.*

*When the current abilities of capable people
can be molded to fit the new competency requirements,
positive, creative tension results.*

market, transforming themselves into grain distributors, food processors, and so forth. They did whatever it took. After all, they were trying to survive.

Today, we can only imagine how the overwhelming changes within those organizations affected their personnel. With new product formulations, new customers, new production procedures, unfamiliar channels of distribution—in effect, new businesses— entire workforces had to refocus and be retrained. Of course, some employees, such as the brewmeister or the champagne master, were out of luck. Their high-priced, highly specialized talents were no longer needed, which prevented them from adapting. You don't need a discriminating palette or a "great nose" in the soda pop business.

Charting a new course always dictates that adjustments in an organization's structure be made. They may not be as severe as those required during Prohibition, but they are important if the new mission is to be accomplished. Naturally, the more profound the course correction, the greater the changes.

At the very least, some of the old job slots will require redefinition. Likely, entirely new jobs or departments may have to be created. Whatever the case, you will definitely demand new worker competencies within your organization. These demands must be met.

In terms of our tension thermostat, ignoring worker competencies will only increase the amount of disruptive tension in the organization. Workers who are in the wrong jobs or who are asked to do new ones without being taught needed skills will experience a great deal of tension. They will increase the tension within the whole system because their lack of competence will affect everyone around them. This is especially damaging if it occurs when you are asking people to commit themselves to a new mission.

In contrast, when the current abilities of capable people can be molded to fit the new competency requirements, positive, creative tension results. This change can be energizing. It's an ideal, but it is what you should strive for at every position. The purpose of this

To understand what the right "fit"
is for any given individual, we have to understand
what motivates people to work.

Reason for working:
People work to obtain their own
desired satisfactions.

Maslow's "hierarchy of needs," describes six levels
of satisfaction sought by all people.
They are physiological, security, social interaction, esteem,
independence, and self-actualization. Each of us is con-
stantly striving to fulfill these needs.

chapter is to introduce you to the seven commonsense steps that will lead you to that optimal "fit." They are not particularly complicated, but time and again, organizations fail to take them. As leaders, we sometimes forget that our organization's goals must be translated into actions that will achieve those goals. Assuring competency is perhaps the most important step toward getting an organization where it needs to be.

The Right "Fit" in the Workplace

To understand what the right "fit" is for any given individual, we have to understand what motivates people to work. As an example, let's take four people with vastly different jobs within an organization: an assembly line worker, an engineer in research and development, the head of the accounting department, and a corporate vice president in charge of sales.

At first glance, their expected characteristics and lifestyles may seem very different. You might assume, then, that their reasons for getting up and going to work every morning are also very different. Fundamentally, however, the *reason* for working is the same for all four: *People work to obtain their own desired satisfactions.*

You are probably familiar with Maslow's "hierarchy of needs," which describes six levels of satisfaction sought by all people. From most basic to most complex, they are physiological, security, social interaction, esteem, independence, and self-actualization. Each of us is constantly striving to fulfill these needs.

When any of these needs goes unsatisfied, we feel tension. To reduce or eliminate the tension, we strive to gratify the unfulfilled need. For example, in our society, the best way we can satisfy our physiological needs is to work for the money needed to satisfy them. In doing so, we move away from discomfort and toward gratification. From this point, we may work to satisfy another, higher need, such as security or social interaction, thereby initiating another cycle of tension.

For the assembly line worker in our example, a salary may be the only major need satisfied by working. Other needs are fulfilled

Common Sense Capsule

The more an individual's personal needs are satisfied within an organization, the greater the motivation to achieve the organization's goals and objectives.

When the "fit" is not there, disruptive tension results.

Enthusiasm abounds because individuals' needs and those of the organization are in line.

away from the job. For the accounting supervisor, a need to belong may be met through working with a group. The engineer could be striving for self-actualization. Finally, in a typical structure, the vice president's self-esteem and drive to succeed might be completely bound up in work.

Of course, we are simplifying the lives of these people to make a point: The desired satisfactions people strive for are always personal. Always. Each of us has a complex set of needs to fulfill.

Whatever these personal satisfactions are, make no mistake, they are not for the greater good of Corporation X. That doesn't mean we *never* work for the greater good of Corporation X. It's just that when we do, it is because some of our own personal needs are being met. Indeed, the more an individual's personal needs are satisfied within an organization, the greater the motivation to achieve the organization's goals and objectives.

Conversely, when someone's desired satisfactions do not mesh with the organization's goals, that individual will first seek to satisfy personal needs and wants before working for the organization's goals. When the "fit" is not there, disruptive tension results.

If personal tension levels get too high, the workers in our example may look for jobs elsewhere. If they stay, their tension may build and manifest itself in dysfunctional behavior and attitudes. They may feel anxiety and stress. Their morale may plummet. They may lose their zest for work and start doing just enough to get by. Their loyalty and trust may disappear as they assign bad motives to every initiative made by their bosses and the organization.

A particularly disruptive variation of this behavior is "anti-organizational creativity," a subtle form of sabotage, as in the oft-told stories of auto plant workers who slip a soda bottle inside a door panel or loose screws behind wheel covers. This kind of activity can be found at any level of an organization, with individuals ignoring the organization's objectives or merely paying lip service to them.

What a contrast to the way it can be—should be—when the fit is right and energizing tension motivates workers. Then dys-

*A major U.S. corporation in the information
and publishing industry decided it had
to redefine its business.*

*They decided their organization needed competencies
far different from those they currently had available.*

*We propose seven commonsense steps that can help
any organization determine whether it has the people
with "the right stuff" to get where it wants to go.*

*1. Determine the competencies required in key leadership
and individual contributor positions.*

functional behavior is minimal. Morale is high. Enthusiasm abounds because individuals' needs and those of the organization are in line.

The Seven Steps to a Perfect "Fit"

Some time ago, we worked with a major U.S. corporation in the information and publishing industry whose leaders decided they had to redefine their business. They had to markedly alter their vision and mission because technology had radically changed the way information was gathered, produced, and disseminated. After careful analysis, they could see that their market was headed in a new direction.

They took a look at their new vision and mission and decided their organization needed competencies far different from those they currently had available. Moreover, they believed that the majority of their area managers—people who had been key contributors to their profits and growth over the years—probably did not have the skills needed for the company's new direction. What to do?

In such cases, we propose seven commonsense steps that can help any organization determine whether it has the people with "the right stuff" to get where it wants go.

1. Determine the competencies required in key leadership and individual contributor positions.

As you clarify or redefine the purpose of your enterprise, it's natural to ask: What work is really vital to the new direction? To do that work, what skills, expertise, and competencies are required? Which have become obsolete? This process will help you determine your staffing and development needs and may cause you to enlarge, dilute, redesign, or eliminate positions. Sooner or later, these needs will be apparent. We suggest you find them before they find you. Out of this process comes a new structure with new jobs or existing positions that have been tailored to your new needs. Various methods of "competency profiling" are available to help you accomplish this.

2. Evaluate potential incumbents within the organization against the required competencies for the new positions, objectively determining the degree of "fit" for each.

3. Identify the incumbents who have the required competencies and those who do not.

4. Divide the "do nots" into those whose competencies can be developed and those whose can not.

2. Evaluate potential incumbents within the organization against the required competencies for the new positions, objectively determining the degree of "fit" for each.

This step involves an assessment of the key people within your organization. This would naturally include individuals who currently hold comparable positions in the company and those who have demonstrated either the ability or potential to hold such positions.

A review of past performance appraisals may identify a candidate's exceptional abilities as well as areas in which some improvement is needed. However, use these reports cautiously; they were based in large part on competencies that may be obsolete or incomplete now. Gather new data from 360-degree evaluations, which can provide more accurate and current information. Testing conducted by organizational psychologists can also furnish insight into how well individuals' skills fit the new competency requirements.

3. Identify the incumbents who have the required competencies and those who do not.

Take an inventory of the competencies that are available to the organization. Ordinarily, very few incumbents will have all of the required skills. Make judgments as objectively as possible while matching the competencies of the candidates with those needed for each job. Where are the gaps? Which strengths are you completely lacking? Which skills are underdeveloped? Where are your weaknesses?

4. Divide the "do nots" into those whose competencies can be developed and those whose can not.

Identifying those incumbents in your organization who do have the necessary competencies also pinpoints the people whose present skills are inadequate for your new mission. However, not every "do not" is a "can not." Many are trainable and can develop the competencies they need to contribute. At this stage of the process, evaluate and identify those people who are developable.

All development has to be **self-development.**

*Staying current or learning a new competency
is ultimately a personal responsibility.*

*The likelihood that workers will learn new ways
of getting things done is influenced
by a number of factors:*

Brain Power
Old Patterns of Behavior
Individual Personality and Style
Rewards

*If the old way of doing something is rewarded
more than the new, which do you think workers will do?*

We must keep in mind, however, that all development has to be *self*-development. In other words, all personal progress and improvement ultimately result from an individual's *willingness* to learn new and more effective ways of doing things.

We can work hard to provide opportunities, inspire success, and design procedures—whatever it takes to get people to learn and grow. However, we cannot do it for them, and this must be communicated. Staying current or learning a new competency is ultimately a personal responsibility.

That being the case, the likelihood that workers will learn new ways of getting things done is influenced by a number of factors.

Brain Power. One indication of intelligence is the ability to take in and use data. Research and testing show that intelligence may account for up to 50 percent of a person's ability to change. "Brighter" individuals are faster learners and more likely to replace old patterns with new ones.

Old Patterns of Behavior. Habits that have been rewarded for years are more difficult to break than less-practiced ones. If something we do has worked for us in the past, we find it difficult to give it up.

For instance, a mediocre golf swing may be holding back your golf game. If you seek help from a pro to correct it, you may find it easier to learn a proper swing if you're a novice with no ingrained habits to unlearn.

Individual Personality and Style. Some personality traits favor learning new skills. Others inhibit learning. Some people are not open to new learning because of rigid thinking patterns or strong prejudices.

In addition, there are ways an organization can enhance the success of any training program.

Rewards. The bigger the reward, either tangible or intangible, the more motivated a person will be to learn. This may also inadvertently work as a negative. If the old way of doing something is rewarded more than the new, which do you think workers will do?

For instance, a new inventory procedure may be instituted throughout an organization. It will take time and patience to learn.

*Performance feedback and tracking methods
answer the questions, "Am I on track?
Am I doing it right?"*

*5. Establish appropriate developmental plans
for those who qualify.*

A particular worker finds that his supervisor has allowed him no extra time to gain the new skills. The worker's reports are late because he's still learning, but his supervisor gripes and fumes. The worker can revert to the old way and finish on time. He does this, and his supervisor is all smiles. Under these circumstances, the worker may never learn the new system.

Performance Feedback and Tracking Methods. It's human nature for people to want feedback about how they are doing. Feedback is particularly important when people are being trained in a new skill. In fact, rewards (or lack of them) are a feedback device signaling the answer to, "Am I on track?" or, "Am I doing it right?"

There are a number of ways to provide training feedback. These include *self-observation*, which require that workers have a very clear idea of expectations so they can tell themselves how they are doing. *Boss appraisal and coaching* is very traditional but certainly effective. With *peer rating*, workers' peers evaluate their learning progress. This is useful in team situations or when co-workers are in a better position to judge performance than the supervisor. *Performance tracking of training events* attempts to measure how successful or valuable formal training is for workers who are learning new skills. Formal *360-degree feedback* gathers performance information not only from the boss but also from peers, direct reports, and even customers. This multirater assessment provides a full picture of an employee's performance and usually overcomes the frequent complaint, "The boss doesn't always know how well I perform."

We will discuss feedback in greater detail in chapter 7. For our purposes here, suffice it to say that without rewards and an effective tracking/feedback program, workers cannot make the course corrections necessary to improve performance.

5. Establish appropriate developmental plans for those who qualify.

You have now determined who in your organization has competencies that can be developed to the levels required by your new

6. *Separate the low developable "do nots" from the organization.*

7. *Use competency standards as the basis for new hires.*

mission. For these, create carefully planned learning programs to help them develop even higher levels of competencies. Don't stop at the "requirement" level—make them reach beyond the minimum.

6. Separate the low developable "do nots" from the organization.

There's no nice way to say this. It is time to separate the chaff from the wheat. Some people can be shifted into positions that more closely match the competencies they possess. They will join the other developable candidates. For the rest, however, who not only lack the competencies you require but also exhibit no interest or willingness to learn, it is time to leave the organization. They will likely never fit.

The information and publishing company we referred to earlier found, after completing this process, that only two of their eight key area managers were in the "developable" category. The rest were outplaced and helped to find other opportunities.

7. Use competency standards as the basis for new hires.

Ideally, you now have an organization where the skills and abilities of every key employee match the competencies needed to carry you toward the accomplishment of your new mission. In the future, you should use your competency model to hire new people in accordance with the new requirements your mission demands.

A Fitting Conclusion?

Putting people in the wrong jobs makes no sense at all. You fail to capitalize on their talents while they fail to get job satisfaction. Their inability to do the work results in destructive tension. Attitude and morale may degenerate, disrupting others.

On the other hand, when you achieve the right "fit" between employees and jobs, the foundation of your organization is established on your greatest strength—the skills and knowledge of your people. In turn, you focus positive, energizing tension where it will

*When you achieve the right "fit" between employees
and jobs, the foundation of your organization
is established on your greatest strength—
the skills and knowledge of your people.*

do the most good by providing your employees with an opportunity to learn and grow. In our next chapter, we'll discuss how to enable these competent workers with the power and authority to do great things.

*The satisfactions of making common sense
a common practice in the workplace is watching
the result when you lower destructive tension and increase
positive tension throughout the system.*

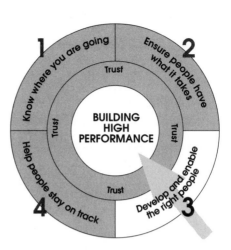

Chapter 6

Develop and Enable the Right People

"Give a man a fish, and you feed him for a day. Teach a man to fish, and you feed him for a lifetime."

—Chinese Proverb

One of the satisfactions of making common sense a common practice in the workplace is watching the result when you lower destructive tension and increase positive tension throughout the system.

So much of the focus in business management today is on overcoming the negativism that seems to permeate the workplace. But we should also set our sights high, focusing on the positive results that can be achieved when a strong sense of direction is coupled with a fully competent workforce. Positive tension doesn't free workers to perform at merely standard or adequate levels. It has the potential of summoning them toward autonomy. It can enable them and allow them to be a collaborative force.

*This chapter will show how careful nurturing
of worker potential can help you tap into the strengths
of people as your greatest resource for achieving
high performance.*

*We begin by establishing certain basics
about how people learn.*

*People most easily learn attitudes and behaviors
that are rewarded and/or not punished.*

*People have an unthinking, automatic resistance
when asked to replace current attitudes and behaviors
with new ones.*

This chapter will show how careful nurturing of worker potential can help you tap into the strengths of people as your greatest resource for achieving high performance. It's the ultimate return on your investment in using commonsense leadership skills.

Before we describe how that can happen, we begin by establishing certain basics about how people learn. Forewarned is forearmed. These are principles we all know, but a reminder will serve as a platform for what follows.

- People most easily learn attitudes and behaviors that are rewarded and/or not punished.

You may remember from basic psychology that this is the "law of effect"; we learn by the consequences of our actions. If a certain behavior is rewarded, we are likely to repeat it. Rewards may be tangible or intangible.

Likewise, if rewards are withheld or taken away for a certain action, we learn to refrain from such behavior. People want to avoid threats to the continuation of their current needs satisfaction, and they will learn attitudes and behaviors that accomplish this.

For example, if workers feel comfortable in their current position, they want to remain there. If they perceive that the organization punishes workers who speak out or offer new ideas, they will probably learn attitudes and behaviors that help them stay invisible, rather than risk being branded troublemakers.

If workers are part of an organization whose leaders reward innovative thinking, new ideas, and resourcefulness, they will have to perform as dynamic self-starters to maintain a favorable status in the organization.

- People have an unthinking, automatic resistance when asked to replace current attitudes and behaviors with new ones.

We said earlier that people tend to resist change. In many cases, it isn't even a matter of having a good or bad attitude. If it were decreed that, starting tomorrow, we will all drive on the opposite

*If it were decreed that, starting tomorrow,
we will all drive on the opposite side of the road,
who would have an easier time of it,
those who have been driving for years or those
who are just learning?*

*When the threat to satisfying current needs is equal to
or greater than the rewards gained from new behavior,
the individual will feel stressful tension and will seek
to maintain the current behavior and reject the new.*

*Strongly held, emotionally loaded attitudes and behaviors
are far more difficult to change than those
not accompanied by emotions.*

side of the road, who would have an easier time of it, those who have been driving for years or those who are just learning? Even with a good attitude, veteran drivers would have a harder time.

For an example closer to business, think of the layout of our typewriter and computer keyboards. They are based on tradition, not efficiency. Studies have shown that we could type faster if the most-used letters were positioned right under our fingers on the center of the keyboard. However, think of the difficulties and stress a changeover to a more efficient keyboard layout would create for the millions who are familiar with the traditional one.

It is always easier to start with a blank slate. Unfortunately, with adults, this is rarely possible. When changes occur and workers must learn new attitudes and behaviors, it is also rarely possible and rather impractical to start with all new personnel.

- When the threat to satisfying current needs is equal to or greater than the rewards gained from new behavior, the individual will feel stressful tension and will seek to maintain the current behavior and reject the new.

This is common sense, but it can be easily overlooked in the workplace. Organizations going through tremendous changes often ask a lot of their employees in adopting new attitudes and learning new behaviors. The organization's expectations may fail to take into account the workers' viewpoint. Yet, think about it. Why should workers be motivated to change under circumstances that say, "You won't be better off doing things the new way, but do them anyway"?

- Strongly held, emotionally loaded attitudes and behaviors are far more difficult to change than those not accompanied by emotions.

You must anticipate the resistance that emotions will create in a learning situation. It may seem more difficult to ask employees to move to an office in another state than to move down the hall. But if people have prejudicial feelings or hang-ups, *who* they will share an office with may be the more relevant and perilous issue. This

Threats to security bring about negative behaviors.

✄

*Effective training efforts fortify the organization's
source of competent people—workers who willingly take
on more responsibility and are prepared to work
with others toward common goals.*

applies not just to obvious emotional topics or issues. We have to take into account any attitudes or behaviors that may carry emotional overtones and thus hinder learning or unlearning.

- Threats to security bring about negative behaviors.

As we've said, this principle is more critical today than ever before. Here is a case in point.

A highly motivated contributor to Corporation X has been a creative, dynamic go-getter for years because his job brings him abundant satisfaction. Many of his life's needs have been met. In essence, he is being rewarded well for the work he does.

Unfortunately, Corporation X has been hit by a series of setbacks. Crushing global competition, customer erosion, loss of patents, and bad fiscal management have caused a high degree of disruptive tension. Everyone is under stress.

Because our worker's security needs are threatened, he resists changes and takes fewer risks. He becomes less creative and has less commitment to change. His new negative emotions and attitudes start blocking the learning of new behaviors that might help his company turn things around, that might spark new ways of dealing with its problems. Now, multiply our worker's reaction by thousands, and you see the plight of Corporation X.

The only way new behaviors can be learned in such an environment is for destructive tension to be reduced. The common-sense leader recognizes how important this is and sets the stage for real learning and positive change to occur.

After all, effective training efforts fortify the organization's source of competent people—workers who willingly take on more responsibility and are prepared to work with others toward common goals.

The Road to Collaboration

Very often these days, a business consultant arrives on the scene amid a clamor for solutions that involve the "empowerment" of an organization's workers. In recent years, the rush to empowerment has been a hot topic. It spread to business from its roots among a

Empowerment is too often perceived as a magic capsule filled with the potent elixirs needed to wipe out every challenge facing today's leaders.

The desire for a quick fix to their problems has pressured many managers into mandating ill-conceived empowerment programs.

Empowerment can actually be a very effective means of dealing with critical business issues of the '90s.

More responsibility and decision making must be pushed down the chain of authority to get the job done.

variety of groups in society. Numerous articles, conferences, and seminars advance the empowerment of women, the poor, minorities, teachers, the elderly, children, immigrants, entire communities, and so on.

Unfortunately, empowerment is too often perceived as a magic capsule filled with the potent elixirs needed to wipe out every challenge facing today's leaders. Our own research with senior managers shows it is not. Nevertheless, the potential benefits of empowerment are so apparent that many organizations embrace the concept uncritically before they lay the necessary foundation for empowerment to yield positive results.

The desire for a quick fix to their problems has pressured many managers into mandating ill-conceived empowerment programs. Then, when the magic potion failed, the result was often disenchantment. A top executive jokingly referred to newly empowered employees as "klutzes with initiative." As a result, many organizations prematurely discarded the tool of empowerment on the pile labeled "Been There, Done That" and waited for the next management fad to come into vogue.

Benefits of Empowerment

What is so unfortunate about this disenchantment is that empowerment can actually be a very effective means of dealing with critical business issues of the '90s, such as increasing productivity, improving quality, enhancing customer focus and boosting profits.

For example, empowerment is a formidable tool for dealing with the effects of downsizing. Today, a typical organization may have removed so many layers of management that a significant number of its workers are performing their duties without adequate supervision. As a consequence, more responsibility and decision making must be pushed down the chain of authority to get the job done.

Another advantage of empowerment is that it responds to a more realistic profile of today's workers. A hundred years ago, typical U.S. factory workers were often poorly educated, non-English-speaking immigrants with an agrarian background. The narrowly

Empowerment can raise constructive tension.

*Increased control brings increased responsibility
and accountability.*

*Empowerment can lower stressful tension by reassuring
competent workers that they are the masters
of their own fate.*

*Leaders who empower encourage the best, saying,
"We know you can do it!"*

defined, oversimplified assembly line responsibilities to which they were assigned made sense, were a satisfactory match to their competencies, and increased the likelihood of their success on the job.

That approach to work is outdated. Today's workers are more capable and better educated, people who are looking for challenges and opportunities for self-realization in the workplace. Ironically, during their off-hours, many who hold "no-brainer" jobs in the corporation use computers to run small businesses. They're teaching night school or resolving complex community issues as members of school boards or city councils. Or they manage large budgets as members of church building committees. Yet, at work, these superb candidates for empowerment are overlooked by their leaders.

Empowerment and Tension

Perhaps the most significant benefit of empowerment is that it provides leaders with yet another method to regulate tension within their organization.

Empowerment can raise constructive tension. Common sense tells us that the more decision-making control employees are allowed to exercise over matters that directly affect their work, the more satisfaction they will derive from their jobs. However, increased control also brings increased responsibility and accountability. The personal stakes are raised for employees. Empowerment challenges workers to be better contributors, especially those whose potential has not been fully utilized.

At the same time, empowerment can lower stressful tension before it reaches destructive levels by reassuring competent workers that they are the masters of their own fate. Instead of an autocratic system that says, "We're watching you to make sure you do things right," leaders who empower encourage the best, saying, "We know you can do it!"

Organizations where empowerment is nonexistent often resemble marionette shows, where the actions of key players are controlled by people far removed from the performance stage. This

*It doesn't make sense to empower
those who aren't ready, and people aren't ready
unless they have the right competencies.*

*The organization must be willing to bolster
the individual's risk-taking attitude by using each
failed empowered action as an opportunity to learn
and build more competence.*

*Some human resource specialists will tell you
that placing limitations on empowered people nullifies
or lessens their authority. In our opinion, it is a lack
of guidance that causes most empowerment efforts to fail.*

style of management instills apathy and resentment in today's employees. It stifles creativity, diminishes problem solving, and fosters disruptive tension—all conditions you are trying to avoid.

Such organizations will always be crippled, limited to the imagination, experience, and brain power of the few making decisions behind closed doors. Yet, out there before them in the workplace is a rich, unacknowledged resource that could flourish if only it were utilized fully.

The challenge is to find a way to empower those resources with sound methods that are likely to produce desirable results.

Ready, Willing, and Enabled?

In its simplest terms, empowerment means to give power or authority to people to help you get to where you want to go. It doesn't make sense to empower those who aren't ready, and people aren't ready unless they have the right competencies.

To build an empowerment program that has a chance for success, people must have "the right stuff." They must have the technical knowledge to do their jobs. They must also have the interpersonal skills necessary to work effectively with other people. They must possess solid decision-making skills to construct and implement sound courses of action. Finally, they must be willing to take risks. The organization must be willing to bolster the individual's risk-taking attitude by using each failed empowered action as an opportunity to learn and build more competence.

Redefining Empowerment

While some human resource specialists will tell you that placing limitations on empowered people nullifies or lessens their authority, we respectfully disagree. In our opinion, it is a lack of boundaries, or more precisely a lack of guidance, that causes most empowerment efforts to fail.

As syndicated U.S. political commentator P. J. O'Rourke reminds us, "Empowerment is what the Serbs have in Bosnia. Anybody can grab a gun and be empowered." A bull in a china

We think **enable**, *rather than empower, is a term
that more accurately describes what is needed.*

✻

*When we enable people,
we give them power and authority.
We also supply them with the means to develop
the competencies and the risk-taking attitudes they need:*

*1. Clearly defined business objectives
2. Guidelines about how far they can go
3. Objective tracking systems*

✻

"Empowerment is freedom within a framework."

shop is empowered. It has total freedom to do anything it wants, and no sane person would dispute its authority. When managers talk about empowering employees, however, we think they have something more productive in mind.

In our judgment, what they have in mind is to enable competent employees to contribute and make more quality decisions at the level where the decision must be implemented.

In fact, we think *enable,* rather than empower, is a term that more accurately describes what is needed.

When we enable people, we give them power and authority. But we also supply them with the means to develop the competencies and the risk-taking attitudes they need to be successful.

For example, competent people must have adequate technical, interpersonal, and decision-making skills to achieve empowerment. Competency assessment can determine whether workers have these necessary skills. Likely candidates can be trained in deficient areas.

We supply the guidance to empowered employees' success in three ways:

1. By making certain they have clearly defined business objectives
2. By providing explicit guidelines about how far they can go
3. By providing objective tracking/feedback systems

While these provisions may seem restrictive to some, remember that workers have maximum freedom within specified boundaries to make judgments and decisions as they see fit. As the executive of a large British retailing chain put it, "Empowerment is freedom within a framework." Furthermore, these conditions are based on solid, commonsense principles. The primary goal of enabling is to help individuals develop winning, successful strategies about the work they do. To that end, we know the following.

- Competent people who have clearly defined business objectives are more apt to make sound decisions.

Everyone answers to someone,
and empowerment does not nullify that.

Real harm can come from misunderstandings
when limits are not set.

You are not introducing empowerment in the workplace as a social or political experiment. While some may regard it as an exercise in democracy, you should have a clear set of business objectives in mind.

The people you enable will make better decisions when they clearly understand the purpose of their work.

Recently the press reported that a group of employees at a tool manufacturing factory in the Midwest was empowered to set its own absentee policy. The objective was not to make the workers feel good or to allow leaders to pat themselves on the back for their benevolence. The goal was to lower an absentee rate that was hurting the bottom line of the business. The employees devised a policy, and absenteeism was lowered dramatically to .0008 percent, in contrast to the national average of 1.8 percent.[1]

- Competent people who know the limits and guidelines about how far they can go are more apt to make sound decisions.

If this sounds like waffling or hedging on the idea of empowerment, it isn't. Enabling workers does not give them any more license to act irresponsibly than the power given to a board of directors by a company's shareholders does. Everyone answers to someone, and empowerment does not nullify that.

Workers need and want the parameters defined. When should they take action? When should they confer with others, such as their boss? It doesn't hurt an empowerment program to spell out limits on decisions that can be made; it strengthens empowerment. We're sure the employees who were asked to set their own absentee policy understood that they could not give everyone 145 personal days a year.

On the other hand, real harm can come from misunderstandings when limits are *not* set. When a decision is countermanded because workers exceeded a limit that was never expressed, they justifiably become resentful and feel the rules were changed after the fact.

Two heads are better than one.

✖✖

*We see the value of teamwork in most endeavors,
even in esoteric fields such as science and mathematics.*

✖✖

*In the past ten years, for instance,
teams of scientists have won the Nobel Prize
for chemistry six times, for physics eight times,
and for medicine nine times.*

- Competent people are more apt to make sound decisions if they also have a tracking/feedback system that permits review, course correction, and result evaluation.

We make better decisions after we have had practice making them and observing their consequences. This is especially true for newly enabled workers who have had very little experience making decisions on the job. A feedback system that tracks their actions provides opportunities for recognition and praise, as well as helpful criticism. We will discuss a number of these methods, including feedback, coaching, and rewards in the next chapter.

Teamwork and Interdependence

"Two heads are better than one." "The whole is more than the sum of its parts." "One plus one equals three." These expressions reflect an almost universal agreement that there are extra benefits to be gained when people work together.

People gravitate naturally to a basic arrangement in which two or more collaborate. Consider just a few examples of solitary activities and how people have turned them into teamwork.

Solitary activities:	Teamwork creates:
Singing	Choir
Carpentry	Barn raising
Playing an instrument	Orchestra
Cheering	Cheerleading team
Nursing	Surgical team
Boating	Rowing crew
Sledding	Four-person bobsled

We see the value of teamwork in most endeavors, even in esoteric fields such as science and mathematics where the stereotype is the eccentric genius who solves problems in a flash of solitary inspiration. The reality is that most "pioneers" making breakthroughs in science and math today are teams that rely on their shared work, insights, and enthusiasms. In the past ten

*As with empowerment,
teamwork has sometimes been embraced too quickly.*

*A good idea may be undermined by pure zeal.
As a CEO put it, a team is "a group that produces
bad decisions faster."*

*Yet the benefits of teamwork are too significant
to be overlooked or discarded because of some
overzealous practitioners.*

*Teams are a natural extension of empowerment.
If empowerment brings out the best in an individual,
team-based work ratchets up the benefits of empowerment
among a whole group of people.*

years, for instance, *teams* of scientists have won the Nobel Prize for chemistry six times, for physics eight times, and for medicine nine times.

Perhaps there was a time when a single executive could solve all problems, evaluate all options, make all decisions, and still have time for a round of golf on Saturday. Gradually, however, it has become apparent that the process of doing business is far too complex for any one individual to comprehend or control. Greater involvement of all workers within an organization is *required* for survival.

Today, the benefits of teamwork are increasingly admired in business management, and a whole teamwork movement has sprung from this enthusiasm. However, as with empowerment, teamwork has sometimes been embraced too quickly. Organizations attempting to maximize their human resources are opting for teams so quickly and completely that a good idea may be undermined by pure zeal. As the CEO of a worldwide rental car company put it, a team is "a group that produces bad decisions faster."

In the rush to exploit the concept, many teams have failed to produce the hoped-for results. As with empowerment, inadequate preparation and poor implementation are largely responsible for the failures.

Yet the benefits of teamwork are too significant to be overlooked or discarded because of some overzealous practitioners. Reports of 30 to 40 percent increases in productivity, or cost cuts of 25 percent are not uncommon in successful teamwork programs. Results like these are hard to ignore.

Real Teams—Real Power

What, then, is the real power of teams, and how can you maximize your opportunity to use them successfully?

Actually, teams are a natural extension of empowerment. If empowerment brings out the best in an individual, team-based work ratchets up the benefits of empowerment among a whole group of people. At their best, teams can develop a kind of ownership culture among workers.

*Teams provide another method
for regulating constructive tension.*

Members feel a responsibility to pull their weight.

*Sharing responsibilities also helps keep
destructive tension in check.*

Traditionally, it may have been the job of someone on the executive staff to admonish the sales force when expense accounts exceeded the budget. Such warnings usually have a fleeting effect.

Imagine instead that five or six salespeople are asked to form a team to institute practices that will trim the expense account budget by 20 percent. Understand, they cannot avoid their mission. They must make the cuts.

In this teamwork scenario, the organization taps into the brainpower and experience of all the team members. The decisions are made at the level of the people who will be most affected by them. More than anyone else, they know where to make cuts that will have the least negative effect on their work. They will have to live with their tough choices. But can't we assume that since they were enabled to make the decisions, at the very least, they will be committed to them in a way they never would have been if they had been handed down from above?

Because of potential benefits like these, some advocates of teamwork predict that by the turn of the century, entire corporations may be run by teams that report directly to the CEO.

We believe teams have a further, often overlooked, benefit. They provide another method for regulating constructive tension. First, constructive tension can be raised because of the expectations of fellow team members. As the group parcels out the work it must do to solve a particular problem, members feel a responsibility to pull their own weight, which means that each individual performs at a higher level than if working alone.

While working in teams raises the constructive tension that results in higher performance, sharing responsibilities also helps keep destructive tension in check. Imagine the pressure an individual would feel if the boss asked her or him to reduce projected expenses for the company by 20 percent. However, when such an assignment is shared, destructive tension is lowered because the individual doesn't feel alone. While team members hold each other accountable for completing their assigned tasks, the responsibility for the assignment *in toto* is shared equally. A group atmo-

*As with empowerment, we have to make sure
that teams have their boundaries clearly defined.*

*They must also have the skills necessary
for effective teamwork.*

*Until everyone had mastered the basics—the blocking
and tackling, the meaning of the quarterback's signals—
until each individual knew specifically what he
was supposed to do on each particular play, the team
would disintegrate and fail to function.*

*That's a lesson that needs to be applied
within an organization.*

sphere and team dynamics can establish a reassuring camaraderie and result in better solutions.

Ready, Willing . . . A Team?

If, like empowerment, creating a team environment is a response to problems created by downsizing, cost control measures, and so forth, then it is important to determine what makes teams successful and what works against them.

As with empowerment, we have to make sure that teams have their boundaries clearly defined. In addition, candidates for team membership should be workers who have already been *individually enabled* by management. They must also have the skills necessary for effective teamwork.

In one of our focus groups, we asked a group that included nine senior human resource executives to define what made for an effective team. Within twenty-five minutes, they identified virtues such as determination, inspiration, competitiveness, enthusiasm, and group cohesiveness—all certainly important. One member of the group, a senior referee for professional football in the United States, remained strangely silent. We asked him what would happen if a football coach emphasized the development of only those team qualities.

"They'd lose every game," he said.

"Why?" we asked.

He replied that until everyone had mastered the basics—the blocking and tackling, the meaning of the quarterback's signals, and so forth—until each individual knew specifically what he was supposed to do on each particular play, the team would disintegrate and fail to function.

Now that's a lesson that needs to be applied within an organization. Teamwork doesn't just happen. You have to make sure the basic individual and group competencies are there!

Without exception, all members must understand the mission of the group and the specific objectives they are expected to meet. As applied to our sales team, they must know that their mission is to lower expenses by 20 percent. The team must break that goal down

*Poorly defined teams, thrown together
with no understanding of their purpose and function,
may never gel as a true team and make collaborative
decisions. Instead, they may become loose cannons,
functioning without considering the impact their actions
have on the corporation or its customers.*

*Teams can fail if they do not recognize that disagreements
can be a source of innovative thinking.*

*Constructive confrontation forces team members
to consider options and alternatives. As a result,
the group is able to generate solutions that
no single member would have found.*

into clearly stated, identifiable objectives, such as reducing entertainment expenses, transportation costs, and lodging charges by specific percentages.

In addition, the team must determine the role and responsibilities for each person in the group. They must know how to track progress toward their goals and how to reward both collective and individual contributions to their success.

Poorly defined teams, thrown together with no understanding of their purpose and function, may never gel as a true team and make collaborative decisions. Instead, they may become loose cannons, functioning without considering the impact their actions have on the corporation or its customers.

People Skills Make Teams Work and Teamwork

The value of teams comes from a kind of critical mass that takes place when a variety of experiences, abilities, ideas, and inspirations are brought to bear on a specific problem. Linus Pauling, a Nobel Prize winner, has said, "The best way to have a good idea is to have a lot of ideas." But the individuals in the group must know how to interact with each other to avail themselves of those combined resources. In other words, they must understand how to arrive at sound decisions *together.*

Teams can fail if they do not recognize that disagreements can be a source of innovative thinking. Members should understand that contrasting points of view are a way of seeing a problem from different perspectives, not necessarily destructive conflict. This type of constructive confrontation forces team members to consider options and alternatives. As a result, the group is able to generate solutions that no single member would have found.

Some might argue that encouraging differences will also encourage hard feelings and division, that by inviting a clash of ideas, suggestions, and solutions from a diverse workforce, you raise the level of tension too high and create disruption. After all, isn't uniformity more efficient?

Granted, uniformity has some appeal. Remember, though, when all individuals within an organization think alike, they

--- Common Sense Capsule ---

When all individuals within an organization think alike,
they might all be right; but they might all be wrong!

In recent years, diversity has become too narrowly
defined as being about gender and race.

In the workplace, diversity can include
a number of constructive differences, such as
differences in thinking style.

In today's highly competitive, global environment,
there has never been a greater need
for positive *diversity.*

might all be right; but they might all be wrong! We have frequently worked with senior management teams who have engaged in what has been called group think, in which differences were submerged to keep tension low and harmony high. Unfortunately, too often this resulted in bad decisions.

The tangible rewards of diverse thinking contribute to the discovery of new and more creative ways of meeting the needs of internal customers, external customers, and stockholders. The 3M Corporation, Hewlett Packard, Levi Strauss, Motorola, and General Electric are all examples of companies who have encouraged expression of differences as a way of stimulating product and service creativity.

Unfortunately, in recent years, diversity has become too narrowly defined as being about gender and race. However, in the workplace, diversity can include a number of constructive differences, such as differences in thinking style. These can enrich an organization and bring to bear more creative resources for meeting the challenge of change and accomplishing the goals of the company. People should be given the opportunity to contribute according to their strengths and differences. Under these circumstances, diversity should be sought out and cultivated. In today's highly competitive, global environment, there has never been a greater need for *positive* diversity.

Of course, team members must have the interpersonal skills to keep their differences from turning into disruptive conflict. In expressing divergent points of view in spirited discussion, members may let their emotions take over and slip into sarcasm, ridicule, or personal attacks to further their arguments. A clear purpose and training in interpersonal skills will go a long way toward avoiding this problem.

Good teamwork also requires that team members understand how to organize and conduct effective meetings. We have all attended bad meetings: meandering agendas, speakers who compete with one another, a meeting that doesn't really end but winds down without consensus on any decisions or plans.

Team members must have the interpersonal skills to keep their differences from turning into disruptive conflict.

Good teamwork requires that team members understand how to organize and conduct effective meetings.

Some form of leadership is present in all groups displaying effective teamwork.

Early advocates of the self-directed teams concept naively flirted with the idea of leaderless teams.

If our sales team holds meetings that are poorly attended, where time is wasted on personal side issues, where one person dominates the discussion while other members go unheard, it won't be able to function *as a team* to arrive at solutions.

Follow the Leadership

Some form of leadership is present in all groups displaying effective teamwork.

Though we have always believed this statement, in recent times, it has come under fire from advocates of so-called self-directed teams, a concept getting much attention in business management today. Early advocates of the self-directed teams concept naively flirted with the idea of leaderless teams but soon learned (either through more reflection or disastrous experimentation) that a clear leader role is essential to the functioning of a team. Latitude exists, however, as to how the role is defined and exercised.

With that in mind, let's take a look at the leadership role in the traditional team, which still makes up the vast majority of existing corporate groups. Whether assigned or elected, the leader has a very visible role—to ensure that the group clearly understands why it exists and what its goals, individual roles, and responsibilities are.

Such a leader also makes sure that each member interacts with other members so all are encouraged to participate, thereby utilizing all of the group's resources. Finally, the leader promotes collaboration to solve the problem or reach the goal at hand. The majority of teams have someone who is responsible for the performance and ultimate success of the team project.

There are also nontraditional expressions of team leadership that emphasize the leader's role as one of a coach or facilitator. While not participating in the work of the group, these leaders help the group consider options and make decisions.

In other cases, a leader may naturally emerge from within the team. To illustrate, a jury functions as a team that has a nominal leader, or foreperson, who is appointed. Quite often, however, a true leader emerges during the discussion of the case. Often, in

In the traditional team, the leader has a very visible role—
to ensure that the group clearly understands why
it exists and what its goals, individual roles,
and responsibilities are.

Nontraditional expressions of team leadership
emphasize the leader's role as one of a coach or facilitator.

Often, in groups where no leader is designated,
someone chooses to become the leader.

In cross-disciplinary teams, members agree to share
or even rotate leadership duties.

groups where no leader is designated, someone chooses to become the leader or is recognized by the members as such. Just observe a playground where the emergence of a leader is a natural occurrence. Among any group of kids, someone usually rises to take charge.

In some cross-disciplinary teams, members agree to share or even rotate leadership duties, perhaps on a weekly or monthly basis. In other cases, various members may swap the leader role back and forth based on their own special competencies. When money issues are on the agenda, the financial whiz takes on the role of leader. When design problems are to be discussed, the engineer takes charge.

Common sense and our own experience tell us that given time, all groups end up with leaders. Without leadership, teams often flounder and lose focus, something fatal to team effort.

Common sense also says that the training of each team member must be more intense and comprehensive as the corporation moves further from traditional team leaders. With a traditional leader, the organization has someone with direct responsibility for making certain that the mission and goals are understood. Someone makes sure that communication occurs, conflicts are settled, feedback is provided, and progress is made.

If a group does not have an appointed leader, then each member of the team must be thoroughly grounded in the technical, interpersonal, and cognitive skills we've discussed.

A Promising Future

In this chapter, we have tried to dispel the hyperbole and unrealistic expectations that have surrounded the concepts of empowerment and teamwork as embraced by some in the workplace today. Our aim is not to cast a wet blanket on the potential of either. In fact, by spelling out what we feel are commonsense conditions that allow both empowerment and teamwork to succeed, we are actually being protective of both concepts. We feel it is unfair to judge their worthiness based on the failure of poorly planned, poorly managed programs.

*Common sense and our own experience tell us
that given time, all groups end up with leaders.*

*By spelling out what we feel are commonsense conditions
that allow both empowerment and teamwork to succeed,
we are actually being protective of both concepts.*

Rather, we have watched well-planned and executed strategies reap tremendous rewards, confirming our belief that everyone benefits when people are given the opportunity to thrive as contributors and to work collaboratively.

Notes

1. James M. Cusimano, "Creating Leaders by Training Managers as Leadership Trainers," *Industrial Engineering* (November 1993): 58.

No coach ever won a game by what he knows;
it's what his players have learned.

It would be ludicrous to send a rocket with a billion-dollar
payload to a destination in space without tracking it
and correcting its course to overcome flaws
in fuel calculations or rocket ignition.

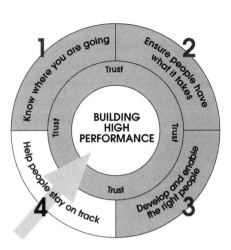

CHAPTER 7

Help People Stay On Track

"No coach ever won a game by what he knows; it's what his players have learned."

—Amos Alonzo Stagg, American Football Coach

Toward the end of World War II, a development took place in the history of rocketry that forever changed the concept of how to hit a target. Previous to that time, every attempt to send a missile from here to there was based on making calculations in advance and hoping for the best once the projectile was fired. If it went off course, it stayed off course. This was true whether shooting a rock from a slingshot or a shell from a cannon.

The new idea was the guided missile. Instead of relying solely on calculations that could later prove inaccurate, this missile had a guidance system aboard that either corrected itself or was corrected by remote control. A more constructive application of the guided missile has steered every rocket launched into space. In fact, it would be ludicrous to send a rocket with a billion-dollar payload

We have compared your organization's mission and goals to a journey toward a target.

Change will continue.
Adjustments must be made all along the way
to shape and improve behavior in order to stay on track.

You will be navigating your organization like a missile,
correcting its course along the way by making use
of continuous, valuable feedback.

to a destination in space without tracking it and correcting its course to overcome flaws in fuel calculations or rocket ignition.

We have compared your organization's mission and goals to a journey toward a target. Let's suppose you take the commonsense steps we have outlined to ensure you have competent people who will get you to that target. You enable them, giving them the means to reach their full potential. You encourage collaboration. You are on track to reach your goal, but what *keeps* you on track?

At the precise moment organizations should take an active role in the development of their personnel, too often they fail to anticipate or plan for the numerous mid-course corrections necessary to home in on their long-range mission and goals. They act as though having an excellent plan at the outset *guarantees* success. The problem is that the changes that prompted the formulation of a plan will not simply stop, frozen like a snapshot in time. Change will continue. For that reason, adjustments must be made all along the way to shape and improve behavior in order to stay on track.

In this chapter, we will show how putting into place a system to monitor and manage performance will serve as your ongoing guidance system. You will be navigating your organization like a missile, correcting its course along the way by making use of continuous, valuable *feedback.*

Feedback—Don't Leave Home Without It!

Like the guided missile, your organization needs feedback. Your employees need feedback. You need it. Without feedback, people cannot improve their performance. In most cases, without it, we can hardly function at all.

Thousands of times a day, feedback tells all of us, from the lowliest plankton to a Harvard professor, what our next move should be. It directs everything from how long to fry an egg to which career to choose.

Common sense says if our internal feedback loop is monitoring our experiences and providing us with information to change our behavior all our waking hours, then it must also play a central role in our performance on the job. Yet our research shows that people's

Our research shows that people's chief on-the-job complaint is they don't get the regular feedback they need.

The signals we receive act to reinforce or reward certain behaviors.

Most of us make use of powerful internal signals to tell us if we're on track.

chief on-the-job complaint is they don't get the regular feedback they need.

How, then, can feedback be put to use both to keep the development of your workers on track and to improve their performance? Before we answer that, let's look at how feedback actually changes behavior.

Why People Are Not Rockets

In response to feedback, for example, a temperature change, the sensors of a rocket don't feel anything. They simply trip switches, responding robotically. By contrast, people react emotionally and psychologically to feedback.

That suggests a principle about feedback among living creatures: *The signals we receive act to reinforce or reward certain behaviors.* (This is what we called the "law of effect" earlier.) The signals provide positive feedback that tells us we are doing something advantageous or right. This kind of feedback, called positive reinforcement, is instrumental in changing behavior.

For obvious examples, let's look at the animal world. Positive reinforcement for animals is simple because they operate almost entirely on the physical level. Most of their behavior is geared to finding food. So every animal trainer has plenty of food on hand to provide positive reinforcement. If you want a seal to balance a ball on its nose, give it a fish when it approximates a step in the right direction. If you've ever taught a dog to sit up or roll over, you know to use treats for a reward. In fact, for animals, this literal "feed" back is so powerful, they can be trained to do almost anything.

Of course, people are different from animals. That's why we don't put cookie dispensers next to everyone's desk at the office. *The feedback signals for humans are not all external physical rewards. Most of us make use of powerful internal signals to tell us if we're on track.*

Consider a basketball player working on her foul shot. What is going on in terms of her changing behavior? Plenty of external signals provide feedback. With each shot, the player gets the infor-

*When people receive positive feedback
from any behavior they engage in, they learn that behavior
and repeat it.*

*By defining our mission, we were able to identify
the competencies needed to reach our target.
These competency profiles define our training objectives.
By devising a development program with feedback
and reward systems that promote the growth
and improvement in the competencies required,
we've created a performance management system.*

mation she needs to improve. This feedback determines the adjustments she makes. As she improves, the feedback tells her she is on the right track, and her reward is the psychological fulfillment she gets from perfecting her skills.

That's why it is not necessary to give her a reward with each successful shot. As she gets better, the player is receiving positive *internal* reinforcement.

It's a commonsense principle we see all around us. This is a need that goes beyond external, physical rewards. Thus we shoot baskets, jump rope, throw darts, paint pictures, juggle, ski, toss cards into a hat, play video games, work crossword puzzles, stand on our heads and, yes, even excel in our jobs.

This tracks with the idea that all development is self-development. While we can initiate programs, offer training, and provide incentives to encourage development, individuals must have a desire to change. Only they can make the effort to learn the competencies needed to perform a job or improve job performance over time.

Moreover, *when people receive positive feedback from any behavior they engage in, they learn that behavior and repeat it.* That's the commonsense foundation for employing positive reinforcement techniques in the workplace. The need to recognize employees' good works, to reward desirable behavior, growth, and personal development is vital to optimize performance.

But how does all this help move us toward our high-performance goals? As we have seen, by defining our mission, we were able to identify the competencies needed to reach our target. These competency profiles define our training objectives. By devising a development program with feedback and reward systems that promote the growth and improvement in the competencies required, we've created a performance management system that moves the people in the organization toward the fulfillment of our mission. Instead of limiting rewards to longevity, loyalty, or other traditional accomplishments, we reward behavior that optimizes high performance.

Broadening the concept of positive reinforcement also has other important implications in today's business climate. Traditionally,

*Traditionally, the standard method of reward
has been a promotion or a pay increase.*

*The two most traditional forms of positive reinforcement
are now precious commodities that must be
carefully allocated.*

Feedback signals may come from external sources.

*The coach is a key factor because research
repeatedly shows that feedback from another person
will speed up the process of correcting
and improving performance.*

the standard method of reward has been a promotion or a pay increase. However, the recent drive to remove layers of management has flattened most organizations to the extent that there are few, if any, positions available to accommodate promotions. Along with downsizing, cost cutting has limited the money available for pay raises. Consequently, the two most traditional forms of positive reinforcement are now precious commodities that must be carefully allocated. Only by expanding the types of positive reinforcement to adapt to the new corporate landscape can we offer people meaningful incentives to develop skills on the job.

The Feedback Role of the Leader

At this point, what else can your organization do to track and improve performance effectively? One more important principle of feedback supplies the answer: *Feedback signals may come from external sources.*

Let's go back to our basketball player. We said she has both external and internal sources of feedback. One external source we haven't mentioned is her coach. An athletic coach can provide valuable feedback in the form of encouragement and instruction. The coach may analyze the player's mechanics and spot a flaw in her movement, tell the player how she is doing and outline a schedule for practicing her skills, or simply tell her to hang in there and be patient.

We know the coach is a key factor because research repeatedly shows that feedback from another person will speed up the process of correcting and improving performance. It's also common sense. It's basically a teaching role. The requirements are that the other person's feedback be *accurate* and *delivered in the right way.* Recall your own inspiring teachers or the most effective supervisors in your career. Wasn't their feedback excellent?

In the traditional workplace, the person most likely to provide feedback is the boss. He or she is certainly who workers look to. We will discuss an innovative variation on this arrangement later. For now, though, let's see how well the leaders in your organization carry out those mid-course corrections for your workforce.

*Whether we're being praised or punished,
we do take to heart our leaders' feedback.*

Suppose an employee is assigned an important research report and turns it in. When asked for feedback, the boss could reply with the following range of responses, all of which we are certain have been frequently offered.

> "If you can't do your job any better than this, you
> should look for other work."
> "Perfect! Fantastic! I love it! Always a great job."
> "I think it was a mistake to give you this before you
> were ready."
> "Oh. Yeah. Fine. But right now, we need to talk about
> all the stuff coming up next week."
> "I'm proud of you."
> "I haven't had a chance to read it yet. I will as soon as
> I can."
> "I congratulate you. How about a drink after work?"
> "Get out your pen and start writing. Page One. These
> figures should go in the back, not the front . . . "
> "Some of it needs more work. Overall, though, it's
> very good. Let's go over the weak spots and figure
> out what to do."

Any of these sound familiar? Perhaps you have your own nominations for the best and the worst thing a boss ever said about your work. Whether we're being praised or punished, we do take to heart our leaders' feedback. Just a few words can make us beam with pride or destroy us for the rest of the day.

Let's look at the types of feedback offered by the four leadership styles depicted in our leadership model. Keep in mind, as we said before, people rarely fit neatly into any one grouping.

Crime and Punishment

Q1 leadership style, if you recall, is autocratic in its approach. This style exercises a tremendous degree of control over others, insisting that things be done in a prescribed way, placing emphasis on results at whatever cost to others. Workers are the faceless cogs that turn the gears of the enterprise.

Q1 feedback is rarely positive. . . .
Instead of being receptive to it, workers cringe.
They feel punished, and stressful tension results.

Lack of involvement and avoidance of conflict
are the hallmarks of the Q2 *leadership style.*
Q2s offer little or no helpful feedback.

A leader operating in the Q3 manner
will avoid confrontation.

This leads to the worst sin of all
if improved performance is the goal . . .
rewarding both correct and incorrect behavior.

Q1 feedback is rarely positive. When workers do something wrong, they are not merely reprimanded. Correction is handled in such a negative way that those exposed to this style learn to avoid the feedback experience. Instead of being receptive to it, workers cringe. They feel punished, and stressful tension results. Psychological research confirms what our common sense tells us: The ability to take in information and learn from it is significantly impaired by this kind of tension.

Hello? Is Anybody in There?

Lack of involvement and avoidance of conflict are the hallmarks of the *Q2 leadership style.* Communication with employees is achieved by quoting policy and company rules or by transmitting directions from above. "My boss told me to tell you . . ." Thus, the Q2 style offers little or no helpful feedback.

Apply this style to an annual performance appraisal. It becomes a meaningless exercise in the hands of the leader adopting a Q2 manner who is apt to avoid any discussion of the worker's performance and may simply check off boxes on a form without writing any helpful comments. Both parties will probably feel uncomfortable at this meeting.

Those who are not hungry for feedback will be satisfied with their "appraisal." Their level of tension stays very low. On the other hand, those who genuinely desire help and guidance to improve weak areas will learn very little. The absence of any meaningful feedback is apt to raise feelings of frustration and destructive tension.

Don't Worry, Be Happy

Next, consider the *Q3 leadership style* of trying to keep everyone happy. In the name of high morale, a leader operating in this manner will also sacrifice a balanced evaluation of workers to avoid confrontation.

This leads to the worst sin of all if improved performance is the goal: Feedback is neither accurate nor on target. False positive sig-

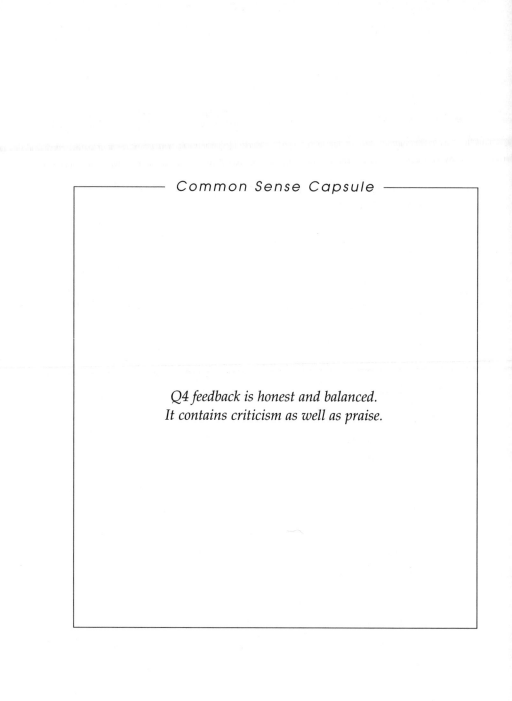

Common Sense Capsule

Q4 feedback is honest and balanced.
It contains criticism as well as praise.

nals are sent out. To keep everybody happy, the leader using a Q3 style rewards both correct and incorrect behavior.

To illustrate the problem, a manager of a national beverage company once told us about a boss who always had a good word for everyone, no matter how poorly employees performed. Eventually, the manager learned to interpret what his boss really meant by adopting the following translations.

When the boss said:	The boss meant:
Good job!	Poor
Well done!	Below expectations
Great!	Adequate
Dynamite!	Beyond expectations
God bless!	Superb!

Like kids at summer camp, workers under Q3 leadership all get gold stars. The cruelty of this false paradise is that some workers accept the inaccurate portrayal as reality and are lulled into performing lethargically, thanks to a very low tension level.

"You Can Do It"

Now, let's turn to the *Q4 leadership style,* which strives to obtain the commitment of workers to the mission and goals of the organization by providing optimal participation, autonomy, and responsibility to people. Q4 feedback is honest and balanced. It contains criticism as well as praise.

This is an important point because many in our society regard criticism as destructive. However, common sense tells us that negative information can produce real improvement. The basketball player may miss many shots in the beginning, but each negative result provides valuable information to use for improvement. When examined, a poor performance can yield constructive feedback on how to change behavior and, thus, provide a positive experience. The difference is that while the Q1 style uses the negative information like a club to beat the worker over the head, a Q4

The leader using a Q4 style is in essence a coach.
A good coach elicits the desire to improve.

We worked with a U.S.-based, multinational
organization where 95 percent of the employees
were rated in the superior to outstanding range.
Yet, the organization was not thriving.

approach turns a potentially punishing experience into a learning experience.

Coaches Develop Winners

The leader using a Q4 style is in essence a coach. Good coaches elicit the desire to improve. They serve as the best outside source of positive feedback yet encourage athletes to develop their own internal feedback and tracking systems as well.

So, the coach in the workplace invites workers to participate in their own progress. Rather than merely correcting them or telling them their deficiencies, a good boss asks employees to analyze their performance and identify where they need improvement. That way, they can create mutually accepted goals.

By encouraging frank and open communication, a boss makes workers feel comfortable about bringing up their ideas and opinions. They know they will be heard and considered. Criticism offered in a Q4 manner deepens understanding and generates a commitment to take corrective steps.

Contrast this result with the Q1 chamber of horrors, the Q2 empty-suit approach, and the Q3 feel-good stroking. Unlike the others, Q4 feedback is worth so much because it meets the criteria. It is accurate and delivered in the right way.

To show the difference this can make to a meaningful tracking system for your organization, we offer our own experience with the kind of "absentee" evaluations that Q2 and Q3 leadership tend to produce. During the course of developing job profiles for our clients, we have found that the traditional employee performance appraisals on file are not very helpful. Why not? Because there is so little accurate feedback in them.

For instance, we worked with a U.S.-based, multinational organization where 95 percent of the employees were rated in the superior to outstanding range. Yet, the organization was not thriving. It was actually foundering on the brink of disaster! Everybody was happy and morale was high, but the competencies and performance required to achieve high productivity were absent. How

A coaching leader raises constructive tension.

*Another type of feedback is often built
into formal training programs.*

*Multirater feedback involves gathering input
from representatives of all the groups who work
with the person being evaluated.*

can this kind of feedback enable workers to change, grow, and achieve the corporation's objectives?

By contrast, a coaching leader uses rapport with workers to regulate the tension thermostat in a healthy way. Such feedback raises constructive tension because the employees play a meaningful, even creative role in seeing things through to their successful outcome.

Other Sources of Feedback on the Job

While we said an immediate supervisor is traditionally the source of feedback for employee improvement, he or she is not the only contributor of valuable information.

Training

Another type of feedback is often built into formal training programs. These can include workshops on topics ranging from finance to leadership to new computer systems. Skills may be taught via traditional classroom methods, computer assisted learning, or hands-on interactive approaches. Vital to any skill-building course, whether for a hard skill or so-called soft skill, is the ability to track and give feedback on learning during the program *and* afterward, during its application in the real world of work.

Realistically, though, the majority of training and development efforts take place on the job. Workers must seek out and be receptive to daily feedback from co-workers and bosses to fully realize the benefits of these learning experiences.

360-Degree Feedback

Workers can benefit from a number of feedback sources, and 360-degree, or multirater, feedback has been proven to provide the full range of signals from others in the workplace. Almost every one of our major client organizations has adopted this as an important source of growth-promoting feedback. Multirater feedback involves gathering input from representatives of all the groups who work with the person being evaluated, often at various organizational levels.

*Some who advocate the use of 360-degree feedback
believe that the information gathered should not
be given to the subject's supervisor.*

*We recommend, whenever possible,
that the boss have access to this information.
If used constructively, the material collected
from multiple sources provides a unique opportunity
for the supervisor to work with the employee
in developing self-improvement goals.*

*Accurate, positive reinforcement accompanied
by discussion of deficiencies unlocks an array
of reward possibilities that goes beyond the job
promotions, salary raises, and bonuses
that are so scarce today.*

How does it work? A person in sales might be rated by his boss, as in a traditional appraisal, as well as by his peers and even a sampling of customers. He is also asked to rate himself. A manager is rated by her boss, as well as by her peers and those who report to her. She also completes a self-rating.

All replies are anonymous, except those from the boss. The employee reads and discusses the evaluation with a supervisor. Together, they work on a plan to resolve any performance issues that surface.

360-degree feedback overcomes the problem of an employee who doesn't value feedback from an immediate supervisor or who discounts negative feedback as merely the result of a "personality clash." It is not easy to dismiss the collective opinion of those who see the worker's performance.

Some who advocate the use of 360-degree feedback believe that the information gathered should not be given to the subject's supervisor. They fear that the raters might not be as candid if they know the boss will be scrutinizing their comments. The worker, too, may object.

However, we recommend, whenever possible, that the boss have access to this information. If used constructively, the material collected from multiple sources provides a unique opportunity for the supervisor to work with the employee in developing self-improvement goals. So, we feel it should be passed along to the supervisor with the full understanding of the person being rated and all others involved in the process.

Moving from Positive Feedback to Career Rewards

Feedback can benefit both your organization and the self-development of its members. Accurate, positive reinforcement accompanied by discussion of deficiencies unlocks an array of reward possibilities that goes beyond the job promotions, salary raises, and bonuses that are so scarce today.

Offering employees new challenges signals that they have mastered the old ones. Special training, increased responsibilities, rotation

*We find that many organizations maintain
a performance/reward system that is
traditional and narrow.*

They reward them for inappropriate behavior.

*When an employee is rewarded after exhibiting
incompetent behavior, what lesson
is learned about that behavior?
Keep doing it!*

*Consider connecting tangible and intangible rewards
directly to the skills and behaviors that produce
higher performance.*

to a more challenging job—these are all positive feedback saying someone is destined for something greater than her or his present role. The granting of more autonomy signals your trust and confidence in a person's abilities. If a job is expanded, it is a signal that an employee has learned new skills that make her or him a more valuable contributor.

Unfortunately, we find that many organizations maintain a performance/reward system that is traditional and narrow. Not only are the leaders unable to reward a sufficient number of people because tangible rewards are in short supply, but they also reward them for inappropriate behavior. They may launch a new initiative that encourages teamwork but continues to reward only individual performance. They may encourage managers to use coaching methods but fail to support the idea with rewards. Or they employ a strict seniority system, rewarding people "across the board" for longevity, regardless of performance. This is positive reinforcement gone haywire. When an employee is rewarded after exhibiting incompetent behavior, what lesson is learned about that behavior? Keep doing it!

These organizations should examine the wisdom of the conventional performance systems that do not reward the new, *desired* behaviors of their workers. They should consider connecting tangible and intangible rewards directly to the skills and behaviors that produce higher performance. It's just common sense that when workers demonstrate improvement on the job, they should be rewarded. That's an effective guidance system in action!

Next, we will see how each of the building blocks we have put into place in the last four chapters will contribute to the one powerful human phenomenon that goes the furthest in resolving the people issues of any organization—trust.

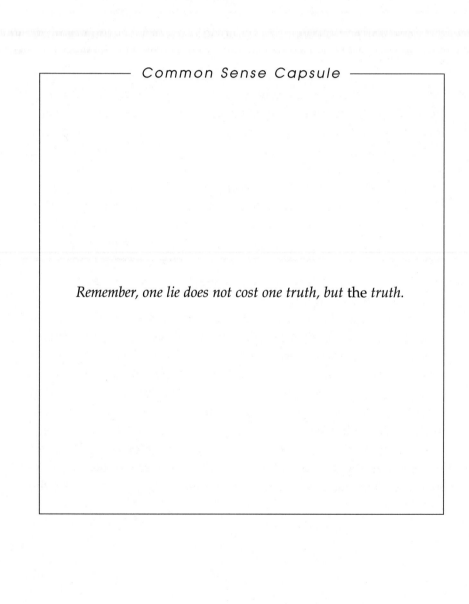

Common Sense Capsule

Remember, one lie does not cost one truth, but the truth.

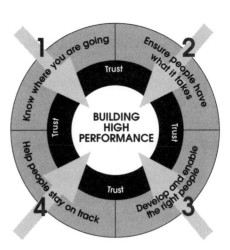

CHAPTER 8

Trust, the Glue That Holds It All Together

"Remember, one lie does not cost one truth, but the truth."
—Friedrich Hebbel, German Dramatist

"I don't mind working here, but I'm watching my backside."

"Dan's my boss. While I trust him, I wouldn't trust the rest of 'em as far as I could throw 'em."

"It's like a family where I work."

"Why should I trust this company? They don't trust me. They watch me like a hawk all the time."

"I think the higher-ups here are trying to do the right thing, but I know my boss is just holding out until retirement."

"I keep my résumé updated. I've seen so many people get the shaft. It could be my turn tomorrow."

"The president gives a speech at the company picnic every year about how we should all pull together, but then we don't see him or hear anything about it again."

*An essential ingredient
for not only improving performance
but also sustaining it during turbulent times is* trust.
We believe it's the glue that holds it all together.

*What provides the breathing room
the organization needs to ride out the turbulent periods
is a reservoir of trust.*

"The first I heard about the layoffs was when I read it in the newspaper."

"I love it here!"

In chapter 3, we made a comparison between organizations burdened by oppressively high levels of destructive tension and those fueled by the energizing power of constructive tension. We noted the irony that, to a casual onlooker, both organizations might reveal strikingly similar behavior: intense activity, workers bustling about, putting in long hours and so forth.

While one group of workers is "frantic," the other is "exhilarated." One group feels dread, the other is turned on by the atmosphere and attitude established in the workplace. That's because where constructive tension is high, workers are motivated to perform, since their leaders regulate the tension thermostat by collaborating with their people and employing the Q4 style of leadership.

But what keeps this workforce so highly motivated over time, willing to accomplish its tasks with zeal even in the face of chaotic economic conditions? An essential ingredient for not only improving performance but also sustaining it during turbulent times is *trust*. We believe it's the glue that holds it all together.

Finding Strength During Difficult Times

Why is trust so essential? Keep in mind that our goal has not been to avoid downsizing or radical restructuring. Rather, our starting point has been that all organizations today operate amid instability. Organizations will never be inoculated against rough times and the forces of change. It's how their people respond to those challenges that counts.

The organization that's a beehive of constructive energy with highly motivated workers is subjected to the same hard knocks as any other. However, what sustains it, what provides the breathing room the organization needs to ride out the turbulent periods, is a reservoir of trust. When an organization and its leaders cultivate trust among the workforce, they can sustain a commitment from

Trust is fragile.

To build a reservoir of trust,
"You have to make three deposits for every withdrawal."

IBM never fired anybody.
In Japan, you worked for Matsushita for life.

U.S. corporations laid off 615,000 employees in 1993
alone. Comparable downsizing has been occurring in
Canada, the United Kingdom, France, and even in Japan.

their workers even though that commitment is challenged from without.

But trust is fragile. Whatever level of trust exists in an organization can be lost if care isn't taken to nurture it. There are limits to how often people will trust leaders if they are betrayed. "Once burned, twice learned" may state it too simply, but it suggests how easily trust can be squandered. A senior executive for a major financial organization told us recently that in order to build a reservoir of trust, "You have to make three deposits for every withdrawal."

In very stable times, the trustworthiness of organizations is rarely put to the test. Until a few decades ago, a time-honored relationship existed between a corporate employer and each worker as an unspoken contract: If you work hard, produce results, and are loyal to this organization, you can look forward to having a job for as long as you want, until you retire.

Both employers and workers supported this state of equilibrium, or at least paid it lip service. Employers could count on their workers' trust as well as respect, loyalty, and gratitude. They often practiced very paternalistic management. For their part, workers put their future in the hands of an employer in order to achieve financial security. They often marched in lock step to the corporate beat in order to get a regular salary, raises, promotions, a health plan, vacations, retirement package—all the benefits to which they were "entitled" as loyal employees. IBM never fired anybody. In Japan, you worked for Matsushita for life.

While this description may never have been the reality for most of the world's workforce, it was held up as the ideal work situation. This type of entitlement "contract" is still longed for as the ideal because it offers stability and security. Many people still desire to be taken care of, even if events over the past tumultuous decade have, in reality, all but obliterated this employer-employee arrangement.

The Times They Are A'Changin'

Corporate America became a different place in the 1980s. Even the largest and supposedly safest havens for workers did not escape

*The current state of instability and change
has contributed to a lack of trust in the workplace.*

*Survey after survey suggests that workers
just don't trust management.*

*Only 38 percent of Princeton workers surveyed
trusted their employers to keep promises.
Imagine if only 38 percent of your friends and family
trusted you to keep your promises!*

*Trust itself is an elusive phenomenon.
One reason is that trust is based on feelings.*

the downsizing that took place in the wake of dramatic change. It didn't stop in the '80s either. U.S. corporations laid off 615,000 employees in 1993 alone. By 1994, they cut staff positions at the rate of 3,000 per day.[1] Comparable downsizing has been occurring in Canada, the United Kingdom, France, and even in Japan. Today, everyone knows someone who has lost a job. The idea of working for one organization for a lifetime has disappeared.

For a workforce aspiring to an equilibrium that is a thing of the past, the current state of instability and change has contributed to a lack of trust in the workplace. Dr. David Noer has written with great understanding about this subject in *Healing the Wounds— Overcoming the Trauma of Layoffs and Revitalizing Downsized Organizations* (Jossey-Bass, 1993).

If it isn't obvious that many employees these days have an arms-folded attitude of "Why should I trust you?" there's plenty of research to back it up. Survey after survey suggests that workers just don't trust management. A *Time* magazine poll last year revealed that 70 percent of workers don't trust anyone at work.[2] *Industry Week* reported that while an overwhelming majority of workers thought it was important for management to be "honest, upright, and ethical," only 39 percent believed that it actually was.[3] Another recent survey showed that 65 percent of middle managers in a sample from the top 1,000 companies believed salaried employees were not as loyal as they were ten years ago.[4] And just last year, a Princeton Survey Research Associates study reported that only 38 percent of Princeton workers surveyed trusted their employers to keep promises.[5] Imagine if only 38 percent of your friends and family trusted you to keep your promises!

Author Warren Bennis sums it up: "Trust, especially today, does not come easily, and it is never given but must be earned. CEOs who believe that trust comes automatically along with the perks, salary, and power are in for some rude surprises."[6]

Common sense tells us that the more trust an organization builds among its people, the more committed employees will be to its goals and bottom-line results. However, trust itself is an elusive phenomenon. One reason is that trust is based on feelings. It can't

*Trust is raised or lowered
by identifiable actions and behaviors.*

*When an organization is erratic or dishonest, breaks its
promises, shuts down lines of communication,
is overly secretive, excludes its people
from decision making, and so forth,
trust is sure to evaporate.*

*Likewise, the actions and behaviors of individuals
will raise or lower trust on the job.*

*Employees also routinely make a distinction
between trusting the organization and trusting
the individuals around them at work.*

be learned like accounting or a foreign language. Yet, our level of trust for a person or an organization *can* be cultivated and altered. We just can't predict or quantify an outcome. Perhaps, that is why little systematic research has been done regarding trust or how it evolves.

How Trust Operates in the Workplace

Trust, like love or faith or patriotism, is a complex human feeling that is difficult to explain, but we do know with some certainty how it operates in the workplace. We know, for instance, that *trust is raised or lowered by identifiable actions and behaviors.*

First, the actions and behaviors of the entire organization affect the level of trust held by its employees. These actions and behaviors take the form of organization-wide rules, procedures, practices, systems, and communication patterns. When an organization is erratic or dishonest, breaks its promises, shuts down lines of communication, is overly secretive, excludes its people from decision making, and so forth, trust is sure to evaporate.

You don't have to work very long in an organization that has lost employee trust before picking up on this feeling. Statements in the company newsletter are met with ridicule and cynical comments. Any change in rules or procedures is viewed as an attempt to take away rights or privileges. People stop believing what they are told and search for the ulterior motives behind any action. Everyone becomes a low-truster.

Likewise, the actions and behaviors of individuals—one's boss, co-workers and direct reports—will raise or lower trust on the job. The same dynamics occur as the result of one-to-one encounters that take place over time. Trust or distrust on this level can be very heartfelt. For instance, the high level of trust generated by an individual leader can create such a strong affinity that employees not only believe in their boss but may also regard him or her as a model to emulate.

Employees also routinely make a distinction between trusting the organization and trusting the individuals around them at work. It's not uncommon to hear people say they admire the com-

Integrity

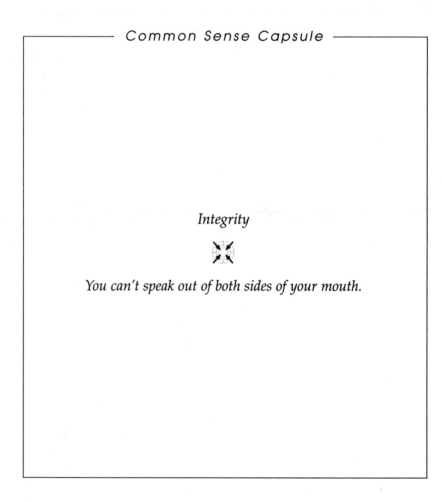

You can't speak out of both sides of your mouth.

pany for which they work but distrust the boss and want to transfer to another division. Or they simply live with the thought that if it weren't for the fine company where they work, they would quit because they don't trust their boss.

Probably more common are workers who trust the individuals around them but distrust the organization. In this case, trust in the boss or co-workers may sustain them. No doubt, many workers feel a stronger bond of loyalty to individuals in the organization than they do for the organization as a whole.

Building the Conditions for Trust

We know from our own observation that trust is raised or lowered in the workplace by certain actions and behaviors, but which of these is most likely to build trust?

Before we discuss the answer, let's agree on what trust is and how it operates by identifying components that make up this elusive quality.

Integrity: An Organizational Example

Rumors were spreading within a worldwide information systems corporation that it would soon be initiating major layoffs. The CEO had not spoken to his employees or the public, but several business press reporters cornered him as he arrived at a social function and questioned him vigorously. He strongly denied that layoffs were in the works and played down the company's fiscal problems. He said that new products in development would help turn the company around; it didn't make sense to cut back on workers. The story was published in national media. Two weeks later, the corporation issued a press release announcing that 4,500 employees would be laid off and five plants would be closed, with new manufacturing plants to be opened in low-cost labor, off-shore locations.

To explain their actions, executives said they had good business reasons for not telling the truth, since they were trying to keep the company afloat and protect the jobs of those remaining. However,

Common Sense Capsule

Reliability

*Reliable people do what they say they will do
when they say they will do it.*

*Two qualities of reliable people
are character and competence.*

there is little doubt about what was sacrificed. Common sense tells us that trust cannot flourish without integrity. Integrity is the cornerstone of trust. If we don't believe what our leaders, our peers or those who report to us are telling us, we will not trust them, no matter what other good qualities they have. Therefore, to build trust, integrity is key. That means being open and honest, meeting commitments and keeping promises. You can't speak out of both sides of your mouth.

Reliability: A Teamwork Example

A team had been formed within a high-tech organization to work on quality control. Too many products were being shipped and later returned with defects, costing money and the confidence of customers. In a very short time, it became apparent that one member from the accounting department was not pulling her weight. While she had agreed to do a cost analysis of the testing and inspection of products before they left the factory, she had not produced any solid figures. She had missed some key meetings, and her reports were vague. The team had become so exasperated that it had reassigned her task in piecemeal fashion to other team members, in effect, working around her.

It's common sense that over time, we stop trusting people who are unreliable. Reliable people do what they say they will do when they say they will do it. They are responsible for not only their own actions but also the actions of their people. They convey by their behavior that they can be counted on.

Two qualities of reliable people are character and competence. Character is the aspect that makes people take responsibility and be diligent in completing tasks fully and on time. Competence is required as well; if people are not qualified to complete the tasks, no matter how much they feel duty-bound to do so, they will probably fail.

The unreliable team member in our example failed either because she lacked the character to take responsibility or she did

Consistency

When workers see organizational actions and behaviors
that are inconsistent with what they have been led
to believe, trust dissolves quickly.

Interdependence

Interdependence is the strongest relationship
component of trust. Unless self-employed or living
on a deserted island, people have to depend
on others for their livelihood.

not have the competence to do the work. In either case, she wasn't to be trusted.

Consistency: An Organizational Example

A large HMO in a major Midwestern state promoted the principle that it would not sacrifice the quality of its patients' health care even in the face of growing costs and a tight profit margin. It produced an advertising campaign that positioned it as a "caring health provider" and had an internal campaign among the staff to drive home these values. Yet, as time went by, many nurses and staff physicians complained that their decisions were sometimes questioned in a way that suggested the bottom line, not patient care, came first. The message and practices were contradictory. They lacked consistency.

Another aspect of trust is consistency. Implicit trust is present at the start of a work relationship. People expect to play by the rules the day they sign up for the job. The policies they are expected to follow, at the very least, suggest a core set of principles and values. When workers see organizational actions and behaviors that are inconsistent with what they have been led to believe are the steadfast principles of the organization, trust dissolves quickly.

Interdependence: A Departmental Example

A department head at a multinational insurance company was required to cut the budget in her department. She had a meeting with three or four of the key people in the department to explain what she had to do. She already felt a strong sense of where she would make cuts but decided to develop additional options before making the final decision. She called a meeting and listened attentively, allowing employees to argue vigorously for their alternative solutions. While she incorporated some of their thinking, she ultimately decided that her original plan would work the best. She explained her decision to her team members. Although disappointed, they agreed to support her plan. Why? They had been listened to, they trusted the boss.

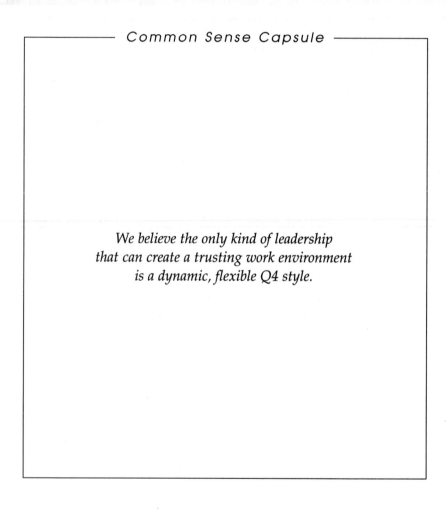

Common Sense Capsule

*We believe the only kind of leadership
that can create a trusting work environment
is a dynamic, flexible Q4 style.*

Whether it pertains to a person, a team, or a whole organization, interdependence is the strongest relationship component of trust. It has been described as a "shared bond." Unless self-employed or living on a deserted island, people have to depend on others for their livelihood. In turn, organizations must have employees to accomplish the work. They must be interdependent because they can't achieve what they need to without relying on others.

Interdependence in work situations requires a willingness to be open with people and to make ourselves somewhat vulnerable. This willingness will depend partly on how many of the other components of trust are present. If another individual, or the organization as a whole, has integrity, is reliable, and is consistent, we will be more willing to let ourselves be mutually dependent.

In our example, the interdependence that existed between the employees and their boss allowed them to feel comfortable in stating their opinions openly, even though their ideas might not have reflected what the boss had in mind. The employees were not afraid of being reprimanded or otherwise placed in jeopardy. The boss understood that her own success was in part due to her ability to marshal the competencies and talent of her people. That means it was in her best interest to be open to her employees' ideas and opinions. The net result was that all parties kept seeking the "right solution," not "who was right."

It's Not Just What You Do, It's the Way That You Do It

If integrity, reliability, consistency, and interdependence are the building blocks of trust, who should the builder be? In his article "15 Ways to Win People's Trust," Perry Pascarella points out the important role the leader plays in building trust: "Trust is won by knowing yourself, letting others see who you are, and being willing to know who they are. All of these things depend on you. None of them depends on the company."[7]

It is not merely the actions you take but also the behavior you exhibit that engender trust. We believe the only kind of leadership

*Those who exhibit the Q2 (uninvolved) and
Q3 (permissive) leadership styles
have a real integrity problem.*

*Even if they display some degree of consistency,
reliability, and integrity, leaders behaving in a Q1 manner
still do not build trust because of their
overriding self-interest.*

that can create a trusting work environment is a dynamic, flexible Q4 style.

Think about it. From our earlier discussions, we know that those who exhibit the Q2 (uninvolved) and Q3 (permissive) leadership styles have a real integrity problem. Their desire to avoid conflict produces evasiveness and dishonesty. Thus, their word is unreliable. Both hold workers at arm's length to avoid interpersonal relationships. And their lack of candor is enough to render them incapable of building a trusting relationship.

Some might argue that leaders who employ the Q1 style may seem trustworthy. After all, no one is more consistent. Ask any worker who has done something wrong. Q1 behavior can also be reliable. You can count on such leaders to push, threaten, discipline, manipulate—whatever is needed to get the job done the way they want it done. Leaders with a Q1 manner might also display integrity.

Even if they display some degree of consistency, reliability, and integrity, leaders behaving in this way still do not build trust. They are disqualified because of their overriding self-interest. They have no stake in building a relationship. It is strictly "my way or the highway." In their eyes, workers have no contribution to make to the organization other than the express discharge of their orders.

On the other hand, leaders who exhibit Q4 behavioral characteristics generate trust. They display integrity by acting and communicating without pretense, criticizing as well as praising with constructive candor. They demonstrate reliability and consistency by establishing ground rules and values that they, too, live by. They involve others strategically in the decision-making process. They aren't afraid to let others see who they are, and they certainly are willing to work at knowing and understanding others.

Practice Makes Perfect

We have identified the qualities that create trust and the style of leadership that can foster it.

That doesn't mean we can derive a formula or recipe that will guarantee trust at the end of the day. Remember, we said certain

All of the actions we prescribe to build high performance also help support a core of trust within the organization.

Know where you are going and be sure your people see what is in it for them to help get you there.

Cultivate the organization and people competencies required to get there so that your people see where their capabilities fit in and where they can make meaningful contributions.

actions and behaviors will raise or lower trust in the workplace. Which ones are most apt to raise trust? What can your organization and its leaders do to raise the level, to allow trust to grow?

The steps we have outlined can create a trusting environment that, in turn, makes it possible for trust to flourish even more over time. Figure 8.1 illustrates the concept. All of the actions we prescribe to build high performance also help to support a core of trust within the organization.

- Know where you are going and be sure your people see what is in it for them to help get you there.

  Employee viewpoint: Not only have they provided the direction, they have also shown what role I can play in their plans. I believe there really is a place for me and I'll profit from working here. I trust them.

- Cultivate the organization and people competencies required to get there so that your people see where their

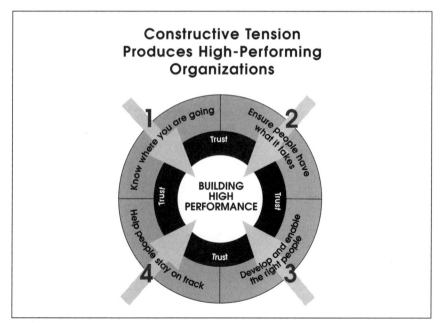

Figure 8.1

Develop and *enable your workers to become more competent. This affords them the opportunity to grow and improve and become more marketable in today's economy.*

Provide the signals and rewards that keep your organization and its people not only on track, but also performing at an optimal level.

capabilities fit in and where they can make meaningful contributions.

Employee viewpoint: They have trained me to do a specific job, but they have also shown me the contribution I will be making to the organization. I have a place here and serve a valuable function in meeting their goals. I trust them.

- Develop *and* enable your workers to become more competent, more proactive, to take more responsibility for their own actions and collaborate with others. This affords them the opportunity to grow and improve and become more marketable in today's economy.

Employee viewpoint: This organization is willing to make an investment in my personal growth. They are expanding my responsibilities and, through training, providing me with new skills that will make me a more valuable employee—even if I choose to work elsewhere. They trust me. Therefore, I trust them.

- Provide the signals and rewards that keep your organization and its people not only on track but also performing at an optimal level.

Employee viewpoint: The feedback I get here—even the criticism—is always put in terms that helps me improve. They are genuinely interested in seeing me develop by keeping me on track. I help produce my own plan for growth, taking responsibility for my own career advancement. I trust them.

Keeping It Going

How can you be sure your organization will take these steps as it goes about its business—day in and day out, year after year? Based on our experience in working with many organizations, we can

Common Sense Capsule

Walk the talk.

Trust is produced when the actions *of leaders demonstrate what they believe.*

Put into place systems and procedures that produce the desired behaviors and actions.

point out five ways to foster trust at both the individual and the organizational level.

1. "Walk the talk."

Although this phrase may seem hackneyed, it reflects common sense. It is fundamental. Do the leaders in your organization say one thing and do another? Talking a good game or writing purple prose that sounds nice in your annual report is not enough. Do you demonstrate in your actions the values or principles that are espoused by the organization?

Consider this statement of James E. Burke, the former chairman of Johnson & Johnson: "The reason we were so successful at Johnson & Johnson was our reputation of trust that went back a hundred years. All previous management, as well as myself, had collectively acted in a way that created a feeling in the minds of virtually everybody that you could trust us. You create the image with a lot of little decisions and actions."[8]

Actions. Trust is produced when the *actions* of leaders demonstrate what they believe.

2. Put into place systems and procedures that produce the desired behaviors and actions.

Take a fresh look at what guides your leaders and the people who report to them. Do you define workers' roles clearly and accurately? Do your systems and procedures ensure that performance measurements reflect what needs to be achieved? Do you administer rewards that enable people to see how they are helping the organization meet its objectives and then recognize their contributions?

It is counterproductive to launch a quality-control program and then only promote managers who deliver quantity. It works against you to launch an effort to work in teams while keeping the old system of individual rewards paramount. The same is true for telling people they will have more decision-making responsibilities without preparing them to use this power effectively.

The idea is that employees take responsibility for their own careers, and companies give them the tools to do so.

In a new relationship between employer and employee, job security is replaced by personal marketability.

Make certain your top leaders articulate a compelling vision.

There's nothing like sincere signals coming from the top to generate an atmosphere of trust that can set the tone for an entire organization.

If you don't have systems and procedures that reflect what *you* really want, people who must work under confusing and, ultimately, unfair conditions will learn to play the game. They will do what it takes to get along, but they won't trust you.

We know that the entitlement culture is mostly a thing of the past and companies can no longer offer job security in exchange for blind trust. Providing competent employees the opportunity to develop and become even more competent can serve to build a different kind of trust.

William J. Morin, CEO of Drake Beam Morin, an outplacement firm that offers help to organizations experiencing downsizing, calls the new agreement "nondependent trust." The idea is that employees take responsibility for their own careers, and companies give them the tools to do so.[9] Cliff Hakim, author of *We Are All Self-Employed*, puts it another way: "Today our world is summoning us toward independence and interdependence—core elements of a new social contract. Independence calls for each worker, on an ongoing basis, to know his or her skills, values, and aptitudes."[10]

Thus, in a new relationship between employer and employee, job security is replaced by personal marketability. Given the opportunity to acquire new competencies, workers learn how to function within a new equation. If they cannot be guaranteed lifelong security on the job, they may grow and empower themselves, gaining job satisfaction and forging this new type of trust in the process.

3. Make certain your top leaders articulate a compelling vision, set high expectations, demonstrate personal excitement and confidence, and show personal support, interest, and confidence in the organization and its people. Leaders must be visible and vocal.

This sounds like a tall order, and it is. Workers may trust the people around them. Their own bosses may behave in ways that promote trust. However, there's nothing like sincere signals coming from the top to generate an atmosphere of trust that can set the tone for an entire organization.

Make sure the organization clearly and often communicates to employees the true "state of the union."

Openness builds trust.
It makes employees partners in the future of the organization.

Does anyone doubt the importance of Lee Iacocca's role in cultivating the trust needed to turn the Chrysler Corporation around? He needed time to get a marketplace response to his new policies and products. He could only buy time by gaining the trust and confidence of his workforce, his creditors, the U.S. government, and the public at large. He did it, not by tap-dancing or equivocating. He expressed his own faith in his organization, his own belief in its ability to succeed; and it was contagious. How much of that success actually came about because of the trust the people of Chrysler felt for their company, as cultivated by their leader?

By contrast, think of the number of organizations that have been poorly served by leaders who have not generated enough trust because they had little interest in being the organization's number-one advocate.

4. Make sure the organization clearly and often communicates to employees the true "state of the union" as well as its goals, aspirations, and achievements.

No one likes bad news, but trust will never flourish in an organization that continually hides its condition from the people who work there. Ultimately, it is operating in bad faith to hide the facts from workers when the enterprise is having troubles. People will probably find out about problems from other sources, such as the grapevine or the news media. Besides, why would the leaders not want to tap into what is potentially the organization's greatest strength, its people, to help solve its problems?

We know of a worldwide producer and marketer of petroleum products that keeps its employees continually abreast of all relevant statistics regarding the company's performance as it compares to competition. This information is flashed on huge electronic billboards strategically placed in employee work areas. They flash the good news and the bad news. Employees know where the company is and how it is performing.

Openness builds trust. It makes employees partners in the future of the organization. Isn't that what you'll need to actually achieve your goals and aspirations? Can a corporation really pros-

Build a history of trust.

*Perhaps there is an appeal to ferreting out
the leadership secrets of Attila the Hun.
We hope you don't think this is the answer.*

per in today's world by trying to drag its people kicking and screaming toward success? Better to enlist their trust and tap into their energy and enthusiasm.

5. Build a history of trust.

Few leaders and even fewer organizations have gained trust instantly. It takes time. Success breeds success, and organizations that begin building a history of being trustworthy develop a reputation that attracts the kind of people who keep the culture of trust rolling. The building cycle is shortened considerably as the newly hired experience a trusting work environment.

These are the actions and behaviors that provide the optimum conditions for trust to grow. Conceivably, an easier way to accomplish long-range goals may exist, some shortcut for thriving during change and uncertainty. Perhaps that is the appeal of ferreting out the leadership secrets of Attila the Hun or someone else far removed from your organization.

We don't think so. We hope you'll agree that commonsense leadership is a far better alternative to get you where you want to go.

Notes

1. "Downsizing," *Florida Trend* (July 1994): 62.
2. Erica Gordon Sorohan, "When the Ties That Bind Break," *Training & Development* (February 1994): 31.
3. Frank K. Sonnenberg, "Trust Me . . . Trust Me Not," *Industry Week* (August 14, 1993): 24.
4. Mitchell Lee Marks, "Rebuilding After the Merger," *Organizational Dynamics* (Autumn 1992): 18.
5. Gillian Flynn, "The Gap Between Workers and Managers Is Growing," *Personnel Journal* (August 1995): 22.
6. Warren Bennis, *Why Leaders Can't Lead* (San Francisco: Jossey-Bass, 1989), 155.
7. Perry Pascarella, "15 Ways to Win People's Trust," *Industry Week* (February 1, 1993): 48.

8. Lynne J. McFarland, Larry E. Senn, John R. Childress, *21st Century Leadership* (Long Beach, CA: The Leadership Press, 1993), 138.
9. Erica Gordon Sorohan, "When the Ties That Bind Break," *Training & Development* (February 1994): 31.
10. Tom Brown, "Life Without Job Security," *Industry Week* (August 15, 1994): 26.

Common Sense Capsule

The turmoil in the marketplace continues.

*Trying to reverse the changes brought about
by technological advances is as futile as trying
to put toothpaste back in the tube.*

*Organizations must continue to find ways to get
the most out of what they have.*

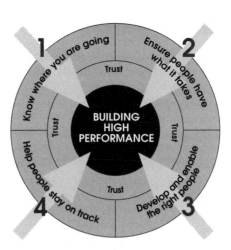

Chapter 9

The Road to High Performance

"You can use all the quantitative data you can get, but you still have to distrust it and use your own intelligence and judgment."

—Alvin Toffler, American Futurist and Author

N othing has changed since you began reading this book. The turmoil in the marketplace continues. The likelihood of it stabilizing any time soon is remote. In a continually shrinking world, global competition will only intensify. Trying to reverse the changes brought about by technological advances is as futile as trying to put toothpaste back in the tube. In a recent report, the American Management Association estimated that 60 percent of the thousand companies it tracks have future job cuts on their agendas.[1] Yet the demands of customers and the expectations of stockholders beat like a drum, sustaining the pressure for better service, lower prices, higher quality, and greater profits.

In other words, organizations must continue to find ways to get the most out of what they have. They must progress toward a

Common Sense Capsule

The ideas we have presented in this book focus on the human side of high performance.

People will always be the most fundamental, developable, and important component of any work organization.

In pursuit of high performance, your leadership will have its greatest impact on the performance of your people.

greater level of effectiveness. They must strive to achieve high performance.

The ideas we have presented in this book focus on the human side of high performance. We understand that to realize absolute high performance, every resource of an organization—technology, finances, materials, as well as humans—must function synergistically and at optimum levels. We also know that besides the numerous daily challenges provided by today's marketplace, organizations must struggle with divestitures, asset management, hostile takeover attempts, plant upgrades—a whole catalog of issues.

However, we believe those organizations that give a high priority to preparing their people to meet the challenges ahead will be the ones most likely to prevail in the future. After all, reduced to its simplest terms, business is collaborative work. It is people performing together to accomplish a common purpose.

People will always be the most fundamental, developable, and most important component of any work organization. Even in today's high-tech environment, a recent statement from the U.S. Labor Department reminds us that almost 75 percent of our national productivity continues to come from people, versus 25 percent from machinery.[2] The performance of an organization's people is still the engine that drives the enterprise. Whatever is expended on behalf of their development will most likely produce the greatest return on an organization's investment of both time and money. In pursuit of high performance, your leadership will have its greatest impact on the performance of your people.

Top Five Reasons the Workers Are Ready

In many of the seminars we conduct dealing with human interaction, one principle we recommend for leaders trying to implement a new idea is to check the receptivity of those whom the change will affect. While the process we advocate requires real time and effort to implement, we believe today's workers are ready. You won't have to wait for them.

According to the Gallup/Inc. poll . . .
the most critical factors bearing on employees'
satisfaction and job performance are that:

Employees have the opportunity every day
to do what they do best
A supervisor or someone at work seems
to care about them as people
Employees' opinions seem to count
Employees had opportunities to learn and grow
The mission of their employer makes employees
feel that their jobs are important

If we had to crystallize all the ideas in this book into one
single postulate, it would be that common sense, your
common sense about human behavior, can lead you as you
guide your organization toward higher performance.

To illustrate the point, let's look at a recent survey of workers' attitudes conducted by the Gallup Organization and *Inc.* magazine.[3] Working adults throughout the U.S. were asked to agree or disagree with thirty-four statements about their jobs, workplace, and job security. Based on an analysis of that data, the magazine published a list of "the most critical factors bearing on employees' satisfaction and job performance." Here, according to the Gallup/*Inc.* poll, are the top five factors that workers want most; after each is an annotation of the applicable recommendations we have offered in our commonsense approach to leadership.

1. "At work, employees have the opportunity every day to do what they do best."
   Enabling, development, right "fit" on the job
2. "A supervisor or someone at work seems to care about them as people."
   Q4-style leadership, coaching, trust
3. "At work, employees' opinions seem to count."
   Enabling, Q4-style leadership, collaboration, trust
4. "Over the past year, employees had opportunities to learn and grow."
   Development, collaboration, enabling, coaching, Q4-style leadership
5. "The mission of their employer makes employees feel that their jobs are important."
   Vision, mission, and values; Q4-style leadership; enabling; right "fit"

It may take some time for your employees to believe in the high-performance process, but there can be little doubt, in view of data like this, about their receptivity to the new idea. Workers are ready to be motivated by their leaders. As the nineteenth-century French politician Alexandre Ledru-Rollin put it, "There go my people. I've got to follow them; I am their leader."

What Will Lead the Leader?

If we had to crystallize all the ideas in this book into one single postulate, it would be that common sense, *your* common sense

Your job is to manage productivity
by regulating the tension level.

Nothing seems to galvanize the efforts of people
working together like a well-managed crisis.

about human behavior, can lead you as you guide your organization toward higher performance. Admittedly, that is quite a promise, but we believe it is also quite justified and supportable. To verify that you can rely on "what you already know," let's revisit one of the fundamental commonsense principles, which we described in chapter 1.

As a leader, think of yourself as the tension thermostat for your organization: Your job is to manage productivity by regulating the tension level.

At first glance, this statement may seem too sophisticated to be basic common sense. However, as we follow the commonsense path of its genesis, see if any of the assumptions are not ones you would make yourself.

Most organizations face unpredictable challenges that must be dealt with expediently and correctly: recalls, price increases, lagging sales, restructuring, new technology, labor troubles, competitor challenges, tight money, fires, or other disasters—anything that threatens the people, profits, or operations of an organization.

Organizations rally to overcome such business disruptions all the time. More than likely, most readers have experienced a period of crisis in their own organizations, times that required extra effort on a large part of the enterprise to see it through.

One thing we learn from such events is that nothing seems to galvanize the efforts of people working together like a well-managed crisis. Handled successfully, a crisis can be an invigorating experience. If you can recall such a time, then you must remember the energizing feeling that occurred when everyone pulled together, reached for a common goal, and performed at a level no one had dreamed possible. Many of the people we talk with remember such a time with a sense of pride. Unfortunately, most report that when the crisis passed, things quickly returned to normal.

So what caused this momentary burst of energy? The vitalizing force was nothing more than tension. Tension produced by the crisis allowed workers to make a direct correlation between their efforts and the productivity, profitability, and overall success of the

Between the apathy-producing lows and the destructive
highs, there is an optimum zone of tension.

Whether dealing with an entire organization,
a department, or a single individual,
every leader must work to keep tension levels
in this high-performance zone.

The methods we have presented can regulate
the positive tension needed to drive your organization
toward higher performance.

organization. If you have witnessed such an event in your organization, then you have already seen the motivating power of tension in the workplace.

What else do you know about tension?

- Whether it's from internal or external forces, tension exists at some level in every organization.
- What differs from organization to organization is the level of tension that exists.
- Between the apathy-producing lows and the destructive highs, there is an optimum zone of tension.
- When regulated appropriately, tension can be the energy source that motivates workers toward peak performance.
- Therefore whether dealing with an entire organization, a department, or a single individual, every leader must work to keep tension levels in this high-performance zone.

The methods we have presented can regulate the positive tension needed to drive your organization toward higher performance. When tension is too low, we've provided methods that will raise it. When tension is too high, we've shown ways to lower it.

Each tension-regulating technique we advocate is based on tested common sense, ideas that have been validated by research or in actual work situations. You can confirm this for yourself by jotting down basic assumptions you believe about human behavior as they pertain to any principle we have stated.

For instance, why is enabling workers such a good idea? What commonsense assumptions can you make about the satisfactions a worker might derive from being enabled? Make your own list, and when you are done, compare it to the one below.

People want to be enabled because they like to:

Accomplish things
Have some control over what happens to them
Feel that their jobs are important
Be included, participate
Feel they are contributing
Think their opinions mean something

Common Sense Capsule

*A great deal of commonsense evidence suggests
that enabling workers is a powerful idea.*

*Rather than have workers who just do the job,
you will be unleashing human potential,
creating circumstances for growth.*

*Your common sense can lead your organization
on the road to high performance.*

Be trusted

Be autonomous

Use their personal judgment, try doing things their way

Learn and grow

You may have thought of several ideas that don't appear on this list, and we may have included a couple that you can add to yours. The point is, a great deal of commonsense evidence suggests that enabling workers is a powerful idea. Furthermore, you can make some commonsense assumptions from the organization's viewpoint that support enabling workers. Chances are, with all the human needs that enabling satisfies, you will get acceptance and commitment to the program once it has been established. You will build trust. Your people will be accountable. Rather than have workers who just do the job, you will be unleashing human potential, creating circumstances for growth. You will have at your command another method of regulating tension. You will be taking a giant step toward high performance.

The Performance-Driven Organization

These are conclusions you can make because through your years of managing and leading people, you have learned a great deal. If you are searching for a new way of thinking to manage the difficulties organizations face today, then we suggest you develop a healthy confidence in the information and knowledge you already have to solve problems and lead people. What is new is what is old. Your common sense can lead your organization on the road to high performance. To help you get started, we have included an exercise that will stimulate your thinking and/or facilitate a discussion with your peers about where your organization is and where you want it to be. (See the Appendix, page 219.)

The journey begins by knowing where you are going. As we said, each step in our high performance model is sequential and interlocking. When the process is completed, everything is linked back to the mission; and every member should be pulling in the same direction. Systems are internally congruent. Everything

Everything stems from your vision, mission, and values. The jobs you offer, the way you train people, the behavior you reward are all determined by this common purpose and direction.

Each of the previous actions contributes to a trusting environment.

stems from your vision, mission, and values. The jobs you offer, the way you train people, the behavior you reward are all determined by this common purpose and direction.

Defining the vision, mission, and values determines the competencies you need. The competencies you need determine your training and development goals. Those goals determine the feedback and rewards you need to keep everything on track. Finally, each of the previous actions contributes to a trusting environment.

What results is a workplace with the right people in the right jobs working to accomplish a set of common goals for an organization committed to constant improvement—all done in an atmosphere of trust. That's as high performance as high performance gets.

It's just common sense.

Notes

1. Karen S. Peterson, "Living in Fear of a Layoff, Boomers Cope with Downsizing," *USA Today* (May 2, 1996).
2. Speech by U.S. Secretary of Labor Robert B. Reich at George Washington University School of Business and Public Management, Feb. 6, 1996.
3. Jeffrey L. Seglin, "The Happiest Workers in the World," *Inc.* (May 21, 1996): 62.

Appendix

On the following pages, we offer you the opportunity to appraise the status of your organization. Using your own common sense, or better yet, tapping the collective common sense of your peers, try to develop a portrait of where your organization is now and where you want it to be in the future.

COMMON SENSE GAP ANALYSIS

1. Recall the graph that illustrates the relationship between productivity and tension.

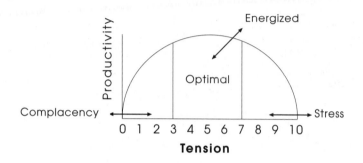

Rate your organization's climate along the above scale (from 0 to 10) during the following time periods:

Where is it now? _____

Where does it need to be? _____

What evidence do you have for the gap, if any, between optimal tension and where you are now?

_____

_____

_____

_____

_____

_____

_____

_____

2. Regulate tension to create a positive energizing force through:

  - Determining a clear purpose and direction
  - Assessing the required competencies
  - Developing/enabling individuals and teams
  - Providing objective tracking, feedback, and reward signals
  - Building trust

Please rate your organization on the following issues.

  - Determining a clear purpose and direction

```
 0   1   2   3   4   5   6   7   8   9   10
```
Vague   Moderately   Very
or   clear   clear
lacking

Where is it now? _____

Where does it need to be? _____

What evidence do you have for the gap, if any, between optimal clarity and where you are now?

_____

_____

_____

_____

_____

What actions need to be taken to help the organization reach its goals?

_____

_____

_____

- Assessing the required competencies

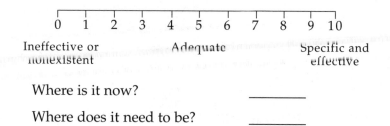

0	1	2	3	4	5	6	7	8	9	10

Ineffective or   Adequate   Specific and
nonexistent   effective

Where is it now?   _____

Where does it need to be?   _____

What evidence do you have for the gap, if any, between optimal competencies and where you are now?

_____

_____

_____

_____

_____

_____

_____

What actions need to be taken to help the organization reach its goals?

_____

_____

_____

_____

_____

_____

• Developing/enabling individuals and teams

```
┌──┬──┬──┬──┬──┬──┬──┬──┬──┬──┐
0  1  2  3  4  5  6  7  8  9  10
```

Sink	Some attempt	Committed to
or	to develop	training;
swim	and enable	supports continual
		improvement

Where is it now?   _____

Where does it need to be?   _____

What evidence do you have for the gap, if any, between optimal development and enabling efforts and where you are now?

_____

_____

_____

_____

_____

_____

What actions need to be taken to help the organization reach its goals?

_____

_____

_____

_____

_____

_____

- Providing objective tracking, feedback, and reward signals

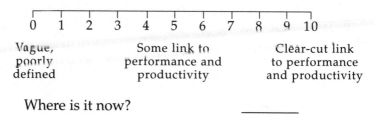

Where is it now? _____

Where does it need to be? _____

What evidence do you have for the gap, if any, between optimal feedback and where you are now?

_____

_____

_____

_____

_____

_____

_____

_____

What actions need to be taken to help the organization reach its goals?

_____

_____

_____

_____

_____

- Building trust

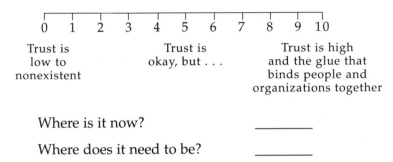

0 1 2 3 4 5 6 7 8 9 10

Trust is   Trust is   Trust is high
low to   okay, but . . .   and the glue that
nonexistent   binds people and
organizations together

Where is it now?   _____

Where does it need to be?   _____

What evidence do you have for the gap, if any, between optimal trust and where you are now?

_____

_____

_____

_____

_____

_____

_____

_____

What actions need to be taken to help the organization reach its goals?

_____

_____

_____

_____

_____

Victor R. Buzzotta, Ph.D.

Victor Buzzotta is chairman of the board of Psychological Associates and a director of People Skills International (UK) and Quadrant, S.A. (France).

Since receiving his Ph.D. from Washington University in psychology and founding Psychological Associates in 1958, he has promoted the use of commonsense methods to select and develop the personnel needed to meet the challenges of ever-accelerating change. He has consulted on change-related issues with senior executives from major corporations in North and South America, Europe, and Australasia. He has authored numerous articles on training and development, as well as co-authored three books on applied behavioral science: *Improving Productivity, Effective Motivation,* and *Effective Selling.*

Dr. Buzzotta led the R&D effort at Psychological Associates when it developed its array of people skills training programs in management, teamwork, and sales. These interrelated programs are used by a broad range of clients in the financial, consumer, and industrial fields.

Robert E. Lefton, Ph.D.

Robert Lefton, co-founder and president of Psychological Associates, is a leading U.S. consultant in sales, management, and organization development. Since earning his Ph.D. at Washington University, he has worked as a consultant with many of *Fortune's* top 500 companies, has served on the faculty of Washington University, and has worked with the Motorola Executive Institute, the ALCOA Executive Institute, and CEO International. As one of the original developers of Dimensional Training, he has conducted seminars for and consulted with several hundred leading corporations in the United States and Europe.

One of Dr. Lefton's major interests is the link between leadership skills and productivity.

Dr. Lefton is co-author with Dr. Buzzotta of three books. He is also a contributor to well-known business journals.

Alan Cheney, Ph.D.

Alan Cheney is an organizational psychologist and is vice president, consulting at Psychological Associates. Dr. Cheney has consulted and taught internationally and, prior to joining Psychological Associates, helped design and implement high-performing teams at Texas Instruments and Air Products and Chemicals. As both an internal and external consultant for thirteen years, he has worked with people at all levels of organizations to identify and fix barriers to organizational effectiveness.

Dr. Cheney has authored and co-authored several articles and a book chapter on increasing productivity within organizations. He has been invited to speak at several international conferences. He has served on a task force for agile manufacturing at Lehigh University and did joint work with Air Products Europe and Cornell University in Europe.

Dr. Cheney holds a Ph.D. in counseling and organizational psychology from the University of North Texas.

Ann Beatty, Ph.D.

As chief operating officer of Psychological Associates' Consulting Division, Dr. Beatty provides a wide range of services to major corporations across the United States. Her responsibilities include executive-level personnel assessment for selection and promotion, executive coaching and development, and CEO team building. Dr. Beatty also provides organization diagnoses to help companies improve performance management systems and maximize their human resource potential. Her area of research interest is the correlation of personality attributes to effective leadership style and management practices.

Dr. Beatty, a member of numerous professional organizations, received her Ph.D. in psychology from St. Louis University.

Index